Praise for *Lead Positive*

"I stood up to take on the *Jeopardy* Challenge and build Watson when the vast majority of technical leaders at IBM stated it was 'impossible,' 'fantasy,' and that 'Ferrucci was a dreamer'—and when the executives backing the project insisted that Watson had to win to save the IBM brand. I look back at what made me successful in the face of such extreme doubt, high stakes, and extraordinary stress, and it was exactly what Kathy Cramer suggests in *Lead Positive*: my ability to honestly reflect and acknowledge challenges and limitations in myself, my team, and current technology, and then summon the courage to focus on what was possible—what could be done with the assets I had in hand and what greatness would be if we built the smartest machine in the world. In retrospect, the ideas in *Lead Positive* enabled me to stay focused, conquer seemingly impossible tasks, and keep the team motivated. I may have acquired them innately, but this book makes the attitudes, ideas, thought processes, and behaviors underlying leadership explicit and accessible to anyone. Had I just dwelled on everything we could not do and our weaknesses, rather than working with our assets, Watson—and its impact on science and business—would have never happened."

   —David Ferrucci, artificial intelligence scientist and
      research lead responsible for Watson, IBM

"The concepts Kathy Cramer has introduced in *Lead Positive* will be as dynamic a tool in the workplace as her previous books about asset-based thinking (ABT). I found ABT to be such a powerful concept that I have distributed copies of her last book to all my employees. I look forward to sharing Kathy's new book with them."

   —Louisa Jaffe, CEO and president, TAPE

"Kathy Cramer's *Lead Positive* connects many previously unconnected aspects of the work of the leader. By showing readers how what they see, say, and do positively impacts themselves, others, and their current situations, she connects their intrapersonal potential with the interpersonal practice of leadership."

   —Peter J. Dean, founder and president, Leaders By
      Design; author, *The Coachable Leader*

"If we all lived by Kathy Cramer's five-to-one principle (five positive thoughts or actions for every one negative), our world would be a better place. Every leader and potential leader needs to read *Lead Positive* to learn all the ways they can increase their positive impact."

—**Barbara B. Grogan,** founder and past CEO, Western Industrial Contractors

"*Lead Positive* confirms what I believe and have experienced as a community leader. Leaders who are geared toward potential and approach their work with abundance are far more likely to rise above the scarcity and barriers that prevent us from moving forward. Kathy Cramer provides us with a personal roadmap toward a very positive future!"

—**Kelly Pollock,** executive director, Center of Creative Arts (COCA)

"The strategies and practices that we have learned from Kathy Cramer over the last twelve years have transformed our work as educational consultants. Now, *Lead Positive* offers everyone the chance to understand effective ways to lead others, building on a foundation of strengths and assets. Kathy has written a compelling and positively practical book for our time."

—**Louise Cadwell and Ashley Cadwell,** cofounders, Cadwell Collaborative LLC

"*Lead Positive* is one of those rare books that can change lives by combining simple, yet profound insights into human motivation with actionable tools. Kathy Cramer has made an immensely valuable contribution to the study and practice of leadership."

—**Bryan Mattimore,** author, *Idea Stormers*

"Just when you thought you had heard the last word on leadership, this revolutionary new book reframes, renews, and reenergizes the act of leading. *Lead Positive* is more than a feel-good book—it equips leaders with a foundation and a compass for being more compelling, more courageous, and more compassionate."

—**Chip Bell,** author, *The 9½ Principles of Innovative Service*

"Yes! There is much more to say about leadership, and Kathy Cramer says it! *Lead Positive* is a life-changing playbook for transforming yourself into an uplifting, engaging, optimistic, magnetic, courageous, and effective leader. Supported by compelling research, brilliant insights, and powerful stories, Kathy provides concrete tools for embracing the mindset and the actions that make you an inspirational, positive force in your organization and your life."

—**Wendy Leebov,** president, Language of Caring

"The most powerful leadership tool is reflection, which leads to positive and deliberative action. *Lead Positive* is a deceptively simple yet high-impact methodology for achieving successful outcomes."

—**Susan Lucia Annunzio,** president and COO, The Center for High Performance; author, *eLeadership* and *Contagious Success*

"Kathy Cramer's asset-based thinking approach to leadership is exactly what our overly cynical, negative, and critical world needs to mobilize our people to perform optimally. A refreshingly new and optimistic perspective on leadership at any level."

—**Molly D. Shepard,** founder and CEO, The Leader's Edge; cofounder and former president, Manchester Inc.; author, *Breaking Into the Boys' Club*

"*Lead Positive* really works to maximize leadership effectiveness. It helped us change our team's mindset from 'negativity bias' to a focus on the positive, and taught us to really listen to each other and to be able to collectively articulate our vision."

—**Mary Alice Ryan,** president and CEO, St. Andrew's Resources for Seniors System

"*Lead Positive* is the owner's manual for ABT Leadership, filled with easy tools and step-by-step instructions to be used every day, in any situation."

—**Gifford Booth,** cofounder and CEO, The TAI Group

"*Lead Positive* is one of those rare leadership books that I am recommending not only to my work colleagues but also to my friends and family. It is one thing to tell someone to lead from a positive approach, and another to give them the tools and methods to put it into action. *Lead Positive* does both and more. It is a must-read for anyone wanting to raise their leadership skills to the next level and have a positive influence on the people around them."

—**Mark Wagner,** vice president, global sales, DuPont

"Kathy Cramer's *Lead Positive* shows you how to get the most out of yourself as a person so that you can be the best leader possible. Her insights and tools on how to leverage the positive dynamics of any situation are critical to making each moment count."

—**Jason W. Womack,** founder, YourBestJustGotBetter.com

"*Lead Positive* is a terrific roadmap for the personal journey of leadership transformation. Kathy Cramer's insightful step-by-step process serves as a guide for putting your leadership intentions into action. As you transform, so will your organization. Mine did!"

—**Joyce M. Dear,** operations leader, Equifax Workforce Solutions

"I found *Lead Positive* to be easy to read, with great examples and guidance of how others have been successful applying asset-based thinking. I found the material on substance, sizzle, and soul to be particularly interesting and helpful."

—**Mark Engel,** vice president, division marketing, Express Scripts

"Kathryn Cramer's *Lead Positive* is a refreshing break from much of today's psychobabble about leadership. *Lead Positive* is a treasure trove of guidance for the kind of authenticity that truly engages people's heads, hearts, and hopes."

—**Rodger Dean Duncan,** author, *Change-Friendly Leadership*

"This book goes beyond the traditional case study regurgitation of best practices and gives us the gift of true insight and practical steps to become better leaders. True to asset-based thinking, it provides us with what we can do instead of what we are not doing."

—**John Sweeney,** speaker, trainer, author, and owner, Brave New Workshop Comedy Theater

LEAD
Positive

What Highly Effective
Leaders See, Say, and Do

Kathryn D. Cramer

JB JOSSEY-BASS™
A Wiley Brand

Published by Jossey-Bass
A Wiley Imprint
One Montgomery Street, Suite 1200, San Francisco, CA 94104-4594—
www.josseybass.com

Jossey-Bass books and products are available through most bookstores. To contact
Jossey-Bass directly call our Customer Care Department within the U.S. at
800-956-7739, outside the U.S. at 317-572-3986, or fax 317-572-4002.

Wiley publishes in a variety of print and electronic formats and by
print-on-demand. Some material included with standard print versions of this book
may not be included in e-books or in print-on-demand. If this book refers to media
such as a CD or DVD that is not included in the version you purchased, you may
download this material at http://booksupport.wiley.com. For more information
about Wiley products, visit www.wiley.com.

Library of congress cataloging-in-publication data
Cramer, Kathryn D.
  Lead positive : what highly effective leaders see, say, and do / Kathryn D. Cramer.
    pages cm
  Includes bibliographical references and index.
  ISBN 978-1-118-65808-6 (cloth); ISBN 978-1-118-84131-0 (pdf); ISBN
978-1-118-83011-6 (epub)
  1. Leadership.   2. Business communication.   I. Title.
  HD57.7.C6953 2014
  658.4'092–dc23

                                    2013040227

Printed in the United States of America
FIRST EDITION
HB Printing   10 9 8 7 6 5 4 3 2 1

I dedicate this book to John Davis,
my husband and business partner,
the light and love of my life.

Contents

Acknowledgments

I am holding the space for a new conversation about leadership. Instead of strategy, market share, alignment, and execution, I want to shine the spotlight on what goes on in the minds, hearts, and spirits of leaders that makes people want to follow them. My question is, "How do leaders use themselves as an instrument to drive positive change?"

There are a growing number of professionals who have joined me in this new conversation by putting this leader's talents, courage, optimism, resilience, and pursuit of a mighty cause center stage. I honor them here:

- I acknowledge and celebrate my partners at The Cramer Institute—Judy Dubin, Peggy Guest, and John Davis—for their unrelenting quest to *see* what is deepest and best in every leader they coach. Their commitment to advancing the principles and practices of asset-based thinking (ABT) is unqualified. Because of their work, leaders are learning to *see*, *say*, and *do* what makes them highly effective.

- Colleen Moore, the director of operations at The Cramer Institute, was willing to *see* my first drafts, *say* what worked and what didn't, and *do* the incredible job of word processing the manuscript in each of its iterations. Thank you, Colleen, for your unwavering dedication and astute feedback.

- I recognize Lori Dixon, an educator who has built her consulting, coaching, and training company on creating ABT applications for administrators, teachers, and students in public and private schools, as well as for leaders and participants in nonprofit youth programs.

- I applaud Beth Chesterton for bringing ABT strategies to coaches around the world. Beth personifies ABT energy, enthusiasm, and commitment. She is dedicated to helping coaches build their businesses, their brand, and their client success stories.

- I am especially grateful for the strong guidance my *Lead Positive* book project has received from my amazing literary agents and savvy editorial team:

  - Anne Marie O'Farrell and Denise Marcil of Marcil-O'Farrell Literary have been consummate collaborators. They embraced ABT and have shaped the *Lead Positive* book project from its inception through the many twists and turns of the publication process.

  - Danielle Goodman has served as my hands-on developmental editor. Her organization, clear thinking, and exceptional ability to coach me in my writing has produced a book that is a good read, as well as a consummate leadership playbook.

- My Jossey-Bass editorial team has given of their time and talents generously and creatively. Clancy Drake got this project off to the right start by providing feedback on the arc and structure of the chapters, as well as a healthy dose of encouragement along the way. John Maas believed in this book from the acquisition phase, and he has devoted extra effort to bringing it to the marketplace on schedule and looking great. Former executive editor, Susan Williams, provided incredible insights that helped me articulate the true value proposition of *Lead Positive*. Finally, Genoveva Llosa, my first editor at Jossey-Bass, was my muse. She helped me find the subtitle of the book. More important, as a leader she embodies the qualities of substance, sizzle, and soul.

LEAD
Positive

Introduction

Lead Positive

What if the leaders in our midst learned to:

See more possibilities than problems?

Say more about "why" and less about "what" and "how"?

Do the courageous thing instead of operating out of the comfort zone?

How much more effective would they be? How many more would they inspire? How much better off would our institutions, businesses, schools, and communities be today and in the long run?

When you Lead Positive, you offer a compelling vision of the future by reframing problems into possibilities and appealing to a higher sense of purpose—a noble and mighty cause.[1]

When you think, speak, and act out of the positive side of the ledger, others feel more hopeful and confident about the future. And when you articulate why your vision is so important to those you serve, they trust and respect who you are, not just your ideas. Then when you take a stand that requires courage and sacrifice, you can rely on their support and determination as you walk together toward a new positive direction.

Turning those "what-ifs" into leadership realities is what this book is all about. My promise to all leaders is that when they shift what they see, say, and do toward what is possible and positive, they will get further, and do so faster. This is true in any situation—even the thorny, difficult ones.

People Follow People, Not Ideas

It's no wonder that public confidence in leadership has been declining; the leaders who know how to lead positive are in short supply. But if you look a little deeper, you will find that it is an overreliance on conventional leadership practices, not the leaders themselves, that are failing us. Conventional leadership emphasizes planning, organizing, setting a direction, developing strategies, and then executing. These approaches are necessary, but they do not inspire. Relying on these practices alone leaves out the most powerful act of leadership: inspiring followers to action. And in order to inspire, leaders must be self-confident and optimistic in all they see, say, and do.

I have found that highly effective leaders approach themselves, others, and the situations they find themselves in from a base of positivity. They take the time to see the good in each moment and share positive learnings with others, creating energizing pauses along the path to goal achievement. They collaborate with others to synthesize disparate points of view into a vision that leverages each person's strengths and speaks to his or her personal motivation. It is easy for leaders to forget that leading is as much about inspiring the imagination and actions of their followers as it is about getting the direction and strategy right. But research tells us that when people at every level feel they are part of creating the vision, their ownership and commitment to execution grow exponentially.[2]

The Asset-Based Thinking Advantage for Leaders

Asset-based thinking (ABT) means to look at yourself and the world through the eyes of what is working, what strengths are present, and what the potentials are. Conversely, deficit-based thinking means to look at yourself and the world in terms of what is not working, what is lacking, and the gaps between where you are and where you want to be.

Our research, corroborated by others, tells us that people have a bias toward deficit-based thinking that follows the old 80/20 rule: 80 percent of the time, we are on the alert for what is not working, what the mistakes are, and what course corrections are needed.[3] Maybe if we're lucky, 20 percent of the time, we are focused on the upside of a given situation and how we can leverage those possibilities.

This tendency to be more sensitive to the negative has an evolutionary basis that psychologists and neuroscientists refer to as the negativity bias, which we explore in chapter 1.[4] For millennia, negative information has weighed more heavily on the brain to ensure survival. For most of our everyday problems and setbacks, this built-in negativity bias aimed at survival is overkill. In fact, when we focus primarily on the deficits, we hold ourselves back. By focusing your attention on what is wrong, you may be able to correct the mistake, but you also risk losing out on unforeseen opportunities, particularly in today's rapidly changing business landscape.

Asset-based thinking is a choice, an intentional way for you to navigate through your day. If you want to be an asset-based thinker, first get to know your strengths and capabilities. Most of us know our gaps and our shortcomings a lot better than we know our strengths and capabilities. Solicit feedback from others to take an inventory of your talents. I call it "reducing the blind spot."

At The Cramer Institute, we encourage leaders to become asset-based thinkers by spending five times more effort and energy on learning what their strengths are and what they have to leverage than they do on their shortcomings. It is a complete reversal of the way we were all trained in school, when we were graded on how many items we got wrong. Teachers, coaches, and parents all thought they were doing us a big favor by focusing on how we could improve, but the research shows that if you want to help someone learn something—particularly anything that is complex or involves dealing with other human beings—you must find a way to move the learner into positive emotional territory (i.e., curiosity, a sense of progress, hope, and confidence). Focusing on what has already been done well is the ticket to accelerating a sense of progress and engendering the thought, "I can do this myself."[5]

While conventional leadership approaches focus on acquiring industry expertise, strategic capability, and operational savvy, ABT is an internal development process that zeros in on transforming what the leader sees, says, and does. When the leader's mind-set zooms in on what is strong, valuable, and possible, what he or she says and does will inspire. In short, this approach helps leaders to shift internally so they can excel externally.

Lead Positive takes the fundamentals of ABT, revealed in my first book, *Change the Way You See Everything*, and turns them into a practical playbook specifically designed for leaders.[6] In this book, I offer tools to leaders for shifting away from a negative bias and intentionally shining the spotlight on the positive, beneficial assets within themselves, others, and whatever situations they may find themselves in.

The Lead Positive Framework: See-Say-Do

The three-step Lead Positive framework helps you shift what you see, say, and do toward driving positive change. The book is divided into three parts that follow this framework. Each provides you with insights and step-by-step practices that build on each other to cultivate your optimism and help you become a magnetic and confident leader. It is best to read these parts in sequence your first time around so you can experience how what you see drives what you say and, in turn, what you say drives what you do. You can think of See-Say-Do as a self-reinforcing system.

I have seen time and time again that when leaders shift their perspective from the negative side of the ledger to the positive side, it creates a positive chain reaction. In part 1, you will learn concrete strategies for focusing positive mental attention on:

- What worked and what you can learn from the past in order to be more effective in the present and more creative in shaping the future
- The positive dynamics in the present in order to take swift, decisive, and effective action toward achieving your goals
- A rewarding vision of the future in order to be prepared for the emerging opportunities that get you there

Connecting what you say to the positive evidence you see is the basis for inspiring and high-impact communication. In part 2, you will learn how to use the Lead Positive communication road map to say it with:

- Substance, by using the assets of logic and conviction to frame a positive vision (the intelligence quotient)
- Sizzle, by using your voice and your stories to engage people's emotions (the emotion quotient)
- Soul, by revealing who you are and why your message is important (the meaning quotient)

Leaders build self-confidence and inspire allegiance by acting intentionally in key, defining moments. By identifying and assessing the behaviors that have helped you create success in the past, you become familiar with your own personal dos for highly effective leadership. The more aware you are of what you do best, the more you can leverage those behaviors. In part 3, you will learn how to use the positive trajectory of what you see and say in order to:

- Respond positively and intentionally to high-stress, high-alert situations
- Find and leverage your signature leadership presence—those qualities of being that make you uniquely effective as a leader
- Drive positive change over the long haul

As you read, you may notice a recurring theme throughout the book: you already know what to do. As a leader, you are already equipped with a unique and effective set of skills to inspire others to achieve a vision. Lead Positive is about first turning your eye inward to see those personal assets—to know beyond a shadow of a doubt who you are and what you are capable of. Making this mental shift will allow you to fully engage your optimism, empathy, and confidence; strengthen your goal orientation; and expand your capacity for learning. Once you can be that solid and authentically positive base, you are primed to see the positive assets of the others around you and of the situation at hand—and to leverage them.

The Lead Positive Advantage at Work

In today's uncertain and chaotic business climate, the need to work together toward a compelling vision looms large. Leaders need to be optimistic and authentic to inspire confidence in their followers and drive positive change. At The Cramer Institute, my team and I have worked with countless CEOs, entrepreneurs, managers, educators, and administrators who have created positive change by embracing the Lead Positive framework. Throughout this book, I offer examples of business professionals we have coached on what it takes for leaders to be effective in challenging circumstances. In addition, I offer examples of public leaders who have ignited passion by—whether they know it or not—embracing Lead Positive principles. I also draw from the latest scholarly research in neuroscience, leadership development, and positive psychology to underscore how optimism and personal magnetism are intrinsic to highly effective leadership.

PART 1

What Highly Effective Leaders See

Zero in on what is working, strong, and possible

1

What You See Is What You Get

This may come as a surprise to you, but we see with our brains, not our eyes. Almost instantaneously, your brain transforms sensory input into thoughts about what you see. Within a few milliseconds of perceiving something, you make meaning out of it.[1] There will always be more than one way of making meaning out of what you see, even if you are convinced you have a clear perspective on what is happening.

The value of searching for the multiple, and sometimes contradictory, facets of what is happening was driven home by New York mayor Rudy Giuliani in the aftermath of the 9/11 terrorist attacks. On the afternoon of the attacks on the World Trade Center, Mayor Giuliani and Governor George Pataki held a joint news conference at the New York City Police Academy. Asked about the number of people who had been killed, Giuliani said, "I don't think we want to speculate on the number of casualties. The effort now has to be to save as many people as possible."[2] By ten o'clock that evening, so many had shown up to help with the rescue operations at Ground Zero that no more volunteers were needed at that time.

In the days to come, Mayor Giuliani used his press conferences to emphasize the courage of the first responders, the generosity and resilience of the citizens of New York City, and the unilateral support of people from around the globe. His focus on what was admirable and heartening was far greater than his focus on what was terrifying.

Note how Giuliani saw and focused on amazing acts of heroism amid the horrific aftermath of the attacks. More important, he communicated the importance and value of that heroism to the world. By biasing his attention toward the positive and possible, Mayor Giuliani led the effort to "turn the worst attack on American soil into the most successful rescue operation in American history," and helped to save an estimated twenty thousand civilian lives.[3] Giuliani instilled hope for the future in millions of people, accelerating the rate at which New York recovered.

The Power of Perceptual Sets

In any situation, from ordinary to extraordinary, leaders can exercise the option to see more of the assets—what is good, useful, and beneficial—than they do the deficits—the bad, useless, and even harmful. That both ends of the spectrum are always present is the truth. What is also true is that each of us (whether we are leading or not) hardly ever sees the whole picture. Instead, we pay attention selectively, zeroing in on only certain aspects.

If I ask you to see the color green right now, you might scan your surroundings and begin to notice green leaves, green hats, green pillows, green accents, and the like. Before I asked the question, the color green was present, but it probably did not stand out in your mind. After I made the suggestion, you likely saw green almost immediately in multiple manifestations. My question altered your perceptual set.

You can think of your perceptual set as your mental predisposition to perceive one thing over another—in this example, the color green over, say, the color red. You can also think of perceptual set in the psychological sense: the expectation that a person will see or perceive something based on prior experiences.

Your perceptual set is one of the most powerful sources of influence when it comes to shaping your selective attention. Many factors can trigger a perceptual set, such as feelings, needs, prior experiences, assumptions, beliefs, and expectations.

Test your own ability to overcome your perceptual set with the following exercise, which I came across in one of my favorite leadership textbooks and have adapted for our purposes here:[4]

Step 1: Read the following sentence several times:
FINISHED FILES ARE THE RESULT
OF YEARS OF SCIENTIFIC STUDY
COMBINED WITH THE
EXPERIENCE OF MANY YEARS

Make sure you have read the text several times before going to step 2.

Step 2: Go back to the text and count the number of times the letter F appears.

How many Fs did you count? Three? Four? Six? Most people do not get the correct answer (six) the first time. The most frequent answer is three. If you did not count six, go back and try again until you find the six Fs.

Why is this counting error so common? The answer is perceptual sets. People most often overlook the three Fs in the word "OF." This happens for several reasons. One is that the letter F in the word "OF" makes a "V" sound in English, not the soft "F" sound as in the words "FINISHED," "FILES," and "SCIENTIFIC." This is an example of an auditory perceptual set: many people hear the words as they read and listen for the sound of a soft F rather than searching for the shape of the letter. People also overlook the word "OF" because it is a "little" word that does not stand out. We ignore the word because of our perceptual set about which words are most important for understanding what we read.

There are strong parallels between this perceptual set activity and the perceptual sets that come into play when you lead. The first lesson in leading positive is to remember that you are always operating out of a perceptual set. The second is that your perceptual set necessarily biases your attention and causes you to perceive only select aspects of a situation.

The clearest example I encountered of the power of operating out of a specific perceptual set occurred several years ago when I was consulting for a division of a large technology company. My assignment was to help prepare engineers with new ideas for products or services to present to an internal panel of executives from the company's Innovation Hub. The Innovation Hub was established to evaluate the merits of new ideas and allocate funding for the development of promising innovations.

So far, so good, I thought to myself as I listened to the general manager explain the evaluation process to me. But what she said next caused me some real concern. She explained that the panel engaged in a process of evaluation that they called "rude Q&A." In this context, being rude meant to "ask as many tough questions as possible to surface any problems or shortcomings associated with the innovation being presented." In addition, it was required that they ask their questions in a tone of voice that was simultaneously "belittling and condescending." This negative tone was designed to test the innovator's internal resolve and ability to withstand harsh scrutiny from a demanding group of high-level executives.

I could hardly believe my ears as I listened to the negative nuances baked into the rude Q&A process. The internal logic of this process and the perceptual sets that were in use went something like this:

- Assume there will be significant problems and flaws that must be surfaced to prevent failures and risky investments (i.e., adopt the perceptual set "interrogate to find the flaws").
- Be sure your tone is rude enough to throw the presenter off guard as a test of his or her gumption and commitment to the innovation (i.e., adopt the perceptual set "intimidate to evaluate").

The rude Q&A process exists in stark contrast to *design thinking*, a more asset-based innovation process developed by the global design consultancy IDEO. Tim Brown, president and CEO of IDEO, defines design thinking as a "human approach to innovation that draws from the designer's toolkit to integrate the needs of people, the possibilities of technology, and the requirements for business success."[5] It relies heavily on the initial step of prototyping to develop and test the potential merit of new ideas.

The design thinking prototyping process requires innovators to adopt the perceptual set of "conversation and collaborations produce the best ideas." This is in stark contrast to the "intimidation" and "interrogation" perceptual sets that underlie the rude Q&A process. Interrogation and intimidation produced anxiety and a win-lose mentality in the minds of the innovators. The innovators I worked with felt vulnerable and uptight as they presented their ideas, and I had my work cut out for me coaching them about how to turn their anxiety into energy. It was as though they believed that this was their one and only chance to have their idea accepted. I believe that this negative dynamic was so unnecessarily stressful that it prevented some staff from stepping up to present their innovations.[6]

Regardless of the perceptual set you commonly operate out of, it is entirely possible to shift in order to perceive the multiple facts that make up any situation. This is exactly what Mayor Giuliani did in response to 9/11: he widened his perspective beyond the obvious acts of terrorism so he could also see the tangible acts of heroism. This was a truly incredible act of leadership—incredible because our brains have a built-in negativity bias that operates in ways that exaggerate the danger or problem, especially in high-stress and high-alert situations.[7]

Our Negativity Bias at Work

Have you ever noticed that you respond faster and more intensely to problems than you do to possibilities? Leaders and followers alike are much more likely to be playing defense than offense. One explanation for this bias toward the negative is that the neural circuitry in the "avoid harm" parts of our brain is triggered faster than the neural circuitry in the "pursue rewards" parts is.[8]

The negativity bias is set up to protect us from harm and provide for our survival. From the perspective of survival of the fittest, it offers a great evolutionary benefit. However, rarely in everyday life do we truly need these emergency, survival-oriented responses. In fact, the fight-flee-or-freeze reactions to situations often put us on the wrong path altogether.

The emergency reaction system is our brain triggering feelings of fear and rage that can make a bad situation worse. Fear prevents the creativity and determined effort it takes to work our way out of a stressful situation, no matter how desperate the circumstances. As President Franklin Delano Roosevelt said in his 1933 inaugural address to a Depression-ridden America, "The only thing we have to fear is fear itself."

When a leader is caught up in negativity bias and is blind to the assets and advantages inherent in a stressful situation, it can trigger a downward spiral. But if, like Giuliani, a leader can see the downsides and the upsides of a traumatic event, danger can be thwarted and progress can be made.

How Your Mind Sculpts Your Brain

Every time you intentionally shine the spotlight on assets— what is positive, valuable, and worthwhile—you change your brain for the better. Donald Hebb, an extraordinarily influential figure in the fields of psychology and neuroscience, theorized that cells in the brain develop strong relationships with one another depending on what we pay attention to.[9] Hebb's law is commonly paraphrased as, "Neurons that fire together, wire together."

Since Hebb's seminal insight, research in the field of neuroscience has confirmed that our thoughts actually do change our brain by creating neural networks that map to the patterns in our thinking. For example, if you are thinking about the benefits associated with a given situation, the neural networks in the reward centers of your brain will fire and wire together to help you learn from and remember that particular positive experience. If you perceive a similar situation in the future, the reward circuitry in your brain will be strengthened by firing and wiring in a similar pattern.[10] Of course, the same process is involved when you perceive negative experiences. When something we perceive as "bad" happens, neurons located in the "avoid harm" centers of the brain fire and wire together. This is how we remember the telltale signs of problems and signals of danger.

What these findings in neuroscience mean on a practical level and in terms of leading positive is that you can intentionally strengthen your capacity for asset-based thinking (ABT). Over time, your ability to shift out of deficit-based thinking will become easier and faster. Your brain's negativity bias will always be in gear to protect you from true harm, but once you calculate that a seemingly negative situation is not life threatening—you realize it is simply a thorny problem or setback—you can train yourself to shift at will into ABT mode. In this way, ABT engages your brain to help you make the best of negative situations. This process of using your thoughts to sculpt your brain is called self-directed neuroplasticity.[11]

Asset-based thinking sculpts neural networks in the "good brain," a term coined by neuropsychologist Rick Hanson.[12] According to Hanson, the good brain's natural state is relaxed, ready for rewards of all kinds, and on the lookout for nurturing relationships. However, the emergency centers of the brain can drown out good-brain functioning, causing us to operate in a stressful, high-alert mode. Given the chaos of our daily lives, by the time we are adults, good-brain activation is limited for many people.[13] But the brains of accomplished meditators have proven that good-brain activity can in fact dominate and trump an overactive, defensive nervous system.[14]

Hanson's research, as well as the research of his colleagues, has proven that anyone can build and strengthen good-brain neural networks with mental exercises that take less than one a minute each. I have included a number of such exercises to prime you for developing an ABT mind-set. You can think of these good-brain exercises that follow as a kind of mindfulness process, a focusing of your full attention on a narrow subject for a concentrated period of time. For the purposes of this book, the subject of attention is something positive—something you find interesting, rewarding, or encouraging—in other words, an asset. You can put these awareness tools into practice right away to find the assets around you and within you.

The See-Think-Feel Awareness Tool

When researchers Bunker and Webb at the Center for Creative Leadership asked successful executives to list adjectives that describe how they felt when they were able to work through tough experiences, their responses were a combination of positive and negative feelings. I have selected seven pairs of experiences from the center's research that represent the positive and negative ends of the continuum:[15]

Negative	Positive
Problem	Possibility
Pained	Challenged
Fearful	Successful
Frustrated	Proud
Stressed	Capable
Anxious	Growing
Overwhelmed	Exhilarated
Uncertain	Resourceful

Reflect for a moment on the negative and positive pairs of experiences while keeping the following in mind:

- Negative experiences under stressful conditions are normal and natural.

- Positive experiences under stressful conditions are possible and even predictable.
- You can create positive experiences under stressful conditions if you shine the spotlight of attention on what is working and what is possible.

The see-think-feel awareness tool is a way to set yourself up for generating the positive feelings you need to stay the course to success. If you are *seeing* the downsides of a situation, then you might *think* "problem" and *feel* "overwhelmed." But if you see the upsides in that same situation, then you will think "possibility" and feel "exhilarated." Think of it as a self-reinforcing process that can either create a virtuous cycle that spawns solutions or fosters a downward spiral that only makes matters worse.

You can use the see-think-feel awareness tool to assess how you are feeling about whatever situation is at hand. If your assessment yields results at the negative end of the feeling spectrum, then you know you have a destructive see-think-feel cycle at work and you need to shift your perspective and create a more useful perceptual set. The see-think-feel awareness tool helps you to spot and correct those negative perceptual sets. To create a more useful perceptual set, use the ASA shift. With a new, more constructive perceptual set, you will be able to discover the possibilities and potential benefits of any tough situation.

The ASA Shift

Altering your perceptual set can be daunting. This "good-brain" exercise helps you to shift your perspective just enough to begin triggering the positive feelings that set a virtuous cycle in motion.

The ASA shift is a mental process with three steps:

1. Acknowledge
2. Scan
3. Act

Think of a situation you are facing right now that fits into the category of challenging or stressful. Maybe an employee is failing, you are way behind schedule on an important project, or the regulators are putting up barriers. Make it a situation you know you could be handling better. Next, follow the ASA steps:

1. *Acknowledge:* Use the see-think-feel awareness tool to identify your negative emotions and trace them back to the negative aspects of the situation that you are focused on. Identify your deficit-based thinking. Acknowledge that the negative aspects of what you see, think, and feel are probably true, but they are not helpful. At the moment, you have a temporary case of opportunity blindness. If you look more closely, you will be able to glimpse some beneficial aspects of the current situation that are also true.

2. *Scan:* Look for the positive side of the ledger. Ask yourself, How can my team or I benefit from tackling this situation head on? Scan for one potential gain or upside. Think about the reward that comes with dealing effectively with the challenge.

3. *Act:* Take one step toward realizing the benefit you now see is possible. Act on that potential gain and feel how it makes the negative thoughts and feelings recede.

Consciously or not, Mayor Giuliani likely used a process similar to the ASA Shift in the earliest hours of dealing with the 9/11 tragedy. His ABT mind-set laid the foundation for the many positive steps to come:

> *Acknowledge the negative:* "We cannot speculate about the deaths and destruction at this time. We have losses greater than we can bear."
>
> *Scan for the positive:* "There must be survivors."
>
> *Act on the positive:* "We must act now to find the survivors."[16]

The ASA shift is not about denying that bad things are happening. Rather, it is a tool to interrupt the negative downward spiral before it gets out of hand (acknowledge), reshape your awareness toward the positive (scan), and begin a virtuous upward spiral aimed at productive action (act). This exercise helps you discover the hidden assets in any stressful situation. Even the gravest and most dangerous situations offer assets that can yield some benefit if we have the determination and courage to see them and act on them.

Resourcing Yourself as a Leader

If you are like most other leaders, you tend to take your leadership skills for granted. You don't often think of these assets, and as a result, they are not top of mind for you. In fact, your own competencies may be buried so deep within your subconscious that you have trouble tapping into them when you need them the most.

Rarely have I found a leader who stops to reflect on the skills that make him or her effective. To the contrary, most mistakenly focus on their shortcomings. A focus on improvement, of course, is valuable, even essential. Without a sincere appreciation of the leadership skills you already possess, you hold yourself back from making great strides.

A deeply abiding sense of the ways you are already effective is a launching pad. Resourcing yourself with the leadership assets you possess activates the circuits of your "good brain."[17] When your good brain is engaged, you are more effective and both relaxed and energized simultaneously. You are better able to see and seek the rewards in any given situation, and you are more connected to the people you need to work with.

This next ABT practice helps to keep your leadership assets in the forefront of your mind:

1. Think about one of your strengths as a leader. Use this list to help get you started:
    - Visioning
    - Strategic thinking
    - Being Decisive
    - Listening
    - Motivating
    - Mentoring
    - Negotiating
    - Problem solving

- Communicating
- Mediating

2. Recall a specific situation when you demonstrated that skill.
3. Let your imagination dwell on that positive experience for thirty seconds until you feel the way you felt that day.
4. Take twenty seconds to visualize that experience soaking into the deepest part of your emotional memory.

I recommend that leaders engage in this good-brain resourcing technique on a regular basis—even daily. I have found that resourcing yourself with your leadership skills not only activates your good brain; it allows you to shift more quickly out of deficit-based thinking into ABT.

When you reinforce good-brain activity, it becomes your home base. Because you visit that mental state so frequently, you know how to return to it when you need to. During stressful times, good-brain activity helps you to muster your best efforts and marshal the efforts of others—in other words, to be a strong leader driving positive change.

The Five-to-One Principle

The work of psychologist John Gottman on what makes for a great marital relationship is by now legendary in the annals of psychological and communications research.[18] Gottman's most robust finding was that in a great marriage, the ratio of positive-to-negative commentary is five-to-one. He and his team of observers were able to predict with 93 percent accuracy which marriages would survive and thrive simply by counting the ratio of positive-to-negative comments.

Since the five-to-one ratio was such a powerful predictor of great marriages, I wondered if it could predict the outcome of any great relationship. My hypothesis was that five times more positive conversations than negative ones will foster trust, loyalty, and engagement in professional relationships. I asked myself, What if leaders intentionally gave feedback to followers about what was going well, what they saw as their strong suits, and what made them believe in the potential of a person? Then my team and I started coaching leaders to do just that.

For over twenty years, we have coached leaders to spend five times more intention and effort on praising people for their proficiencies and the progress they make than they do on criticizing poor performance. The positive impact of this simple yet powerful form of feedback has shown measurable results in myriad ways.

The most important principle to remember when you implement the five-to-one feedback process is to link your praise to the skills and effort that drive the results you want. For example, if you want to see an increase in customer satisfaction, be on the lookout for the communication skills that make customers feel heard and served. Call centers present particularly challenging conditions for customer service representatives. Customers often call in a bad mood because they have a problem or complaint. In our work with call center professionals, we evaluate what kind of communication techniques already work well. Next, we develop new responses and questions in collaboration with the customer service representatives so that they feel ownership in the new communication approaches. Then the old and new best practice communications become the focal point for supervisor praise and recognition. In one of our consulting engagements, customer satisfaction ratings increased ninety basis points just three months after initiating a five-to-one feedback process that targeted best practice communications.[19]

The next section offers you insights into how you can put the five-to-one principle to work to increase loyalty among employees and customers.

Equifax Workforce Solutions

Bob Austin, vice president of operations at Equifax Workforce Solutions, a global provider of human resource, data, and analytics services, came to The Cramer Institute with the business goal of increasing client loyalty from 97 to 99 percent. This 2 percent increase in client retention was worth significant revenue to the company annually. Bob also had a goal of enhancing the level of employee engagement. He believed that if employees were more engaged, they would work harder to satisfy their customers, reducing the likelihood that customers would leave. My team and I helped create a Lead Positive process that would simultaneously increase employee engagement and drive customer retention. Here is how it worked.

Step 1: Share the goals at every level of the organization. The initial step involved socializing the two goals through conversations with Bob's leadership team and then with people at all levels of the organization. My team spoke with the leadership team; in turn, the leaders held meetings made up of ten to fifteen employees to communicate the two-pronged effort of raising engagement and increasing client retention. They also asked employees to describe the new behaviors that would be necessary to achieve the goals. The leaders concentrated on being enthusiastic, showing their confidence in the merits of the goals, and listening deeply to the input of the groups.

Step 2: Identify key behaviors to drive success. Next, my team and I analyzed the data from the leader and employee meetings. What we found surprised us. Not only was there overwhelming enthusiasm for the goals, there were also remarkable similarities in the recommended behavior changes deemed necessary to achieve them. Five key new ABT behaviors were identified:

1. Appreciate positive effort and outcomes.
2. Reveal the "why" behind the "what."
3. Build enthusiasm and energy.
4. Shift from negative to positive.
5. Step up with solutions.

In the case of both employee engagement and client retention, the number-one ranked behavior was "appreciate positive effort." The majority of employees reported that they rarely, if ever, received positive reinforcement for their good efforts; the only feedback they received pointed out mistakes and shortcomings. They made it clear that if managers would tell them when they were doing well, that shift alone would make the difference between "just coming to work" and being excited about contributing to the success of their teams.

Step 3: Put positivity to action. The supervisors and managers agreed to make appreciating positive effort a top priority using the five-to-one principle. In turn, the employees agreed to express appreciation for clients' positive behavior—for example, when they met a deadline, or implemented a new process, or returned an e-mail promptly.

After only one month of the five-to-one appreciative feedback implementation, Bob reported on the initial success: "Our managers and supervisors have said they can't believe the huge, positive difference in attitude and effort initiating this one change has made. And it takes virtually no extra time. It's just about remembering to say out loud the positive effort and outcomes they see. In several offices, it's already become a competition to see how much clients notice and thank their employee contact person for their praise!" After three months, the company's client loyalty metric rose from 97 to 98 percent; within nine months, it rose to 99 percent, achieving the goal of the ABT initiative.

Let's step back for a moment and reflect on what it takes to be able to give five times more positive feedback than negative. The starting point is in what you see. A leader literally has to be able to see the positive actions, capabilities, and potential in people before he or she can give anyone positive feedback. What you see in others truly forms the foundation for what you get from them.

In part 2, we explore how ABT can help you communicate in positive ways that inspire and motivate. For now, focus on seeing what others bring to the table and giving feedback about what you value most. Try cultivating the five-to-one habit for twenty-one days. Note what happens as a result. Your ability to focus on the assets present in others is the single most important thing you can do to build a high-performing organization full of highly engaged people.

The Third Way

In the previous ABT exercises in this chapter, I emphasized the importance of:

- Focusing more on what you stand to gain in any situation than what you stand to lose
- Seeing your strengths in greater measure than you see your weaknesses
- Observing the best efforts and attitudes of people around you five times more often than you notice their shortcomings

These are tried-and-true ways of becoming an asset-based leader.

When we encounter something or someone, we tend to make judgments that lean in one direction or another along the continuum of good to bad, pleasant to unpleasant, or asset to deficit. In each exercise so far, I have offered ways of dealing with these polar opposite ends of our thought spectrum. What I want you to think about now is how ABT can also get you out of the bind of interpreting everything along this binary (good-bad) continuum.

Asset-based thinking can help you rise above a specific situation or condition in order to make a positive meta-interpretation—one that supersedes our tendency to make positive or negative judgments, and creates a third way of seeing something. Think about what you saw or heard about the first debate between President Barack Obama and Republican presidential nominee Mitt Romney during the 2012 US presidential campaign. Every pundit, friend, colleague, and family member I know was talking about who won and who lost. You probably have your own opinion about who came out on top, but set that aside for a moment.

The Sunday morning after the debate, I heard commentator Ben Stein make a meta-interpretation—one that rose above the binary bounds of good-bad, right-left, winner-loser: "In a campaign that's been alternately boring and nasty, this was a night of civility, information, and genuine learning about the men who might be our President . . . No hatred, no talk of punishment, just a wish to make something great even greater."[20]

Stein did not view the debate in terms of which candidate won. He found a more powerful way of interpreting the event. While everyone else was busy deciding whom they liked or did not like, Stein rose above that plane and landed on a different one altogether. He saw evidence that made him proud and hopeful about the future of American politics.

Recently, Dale, a business leader who had just been promoted, came to see me because he was at loggerheads with a colleague. He described the standoff this way:[21]

I have to have my colleague's cooperation because our functions are interdependent. If she fails, I fail. If she succeeds, I succeed. This person refuses to work with me on anything. She fights to get control over

31

my projects and people. She is disrespectful and
dishonest. She lies about what I have done or not
done to my face, to my employees, and to our boss. I
have to fix this, but nothing I have tried so far has
worked. My boss is looking to me to fix the situation.
He is sick and tired of the infighting and wants me
to fix the relationship once and for all.

It is easy to see the bind Dale was in. Just as in the presidential debate, Dale's boss and the employees he managed were looking on and judging. And at that moment, he was convinced that everyone (including himself) thought he was the loser.

To help Dale out of this no-win bind, we started with the see-think-feel awareness tool. Dale described his current see-think-feel cycle this way:

I *see* my colleague telling lies, arguing with me in
front of our boss and employees, failing to keep her
promises and missing key meetings.

I *think* she wants more power and control. She wants
to sabotage my success and undermine my reputation.
She will do anything to keep the conflict going.

I *feel* frustrated, angry with her, and extremely
disappointed in myself for not knowing how to fix
the situation.

As we stepped back to assess the situation, we decided the trap might be Dale's assumptions about what it meant to "fix the situation." Dale's career had skyrocketed in large measure due to his exceptional ability to relate to people. He saw himself as a people person who inspired his team to do and be more than they ever thought they were capable of. No wonder Dale was stymied by his colleague who refused to relate.

I asked Dale to work with me to redefine "fix the situation," to find a third way out of the bind. What if "fix the situation" did not mean fix the relationship? What if it meant simply finding new ways of getting work done regardless of how the colleague was behaving? And what if Dale could view his colleague's inability or unwillingness to relate with compassion rather than with anger toward her and with disappointment in himself?

These new perspectives triggered ABT on Dale's part; it was his way of finding a third way out of the big bind. Dale's redefinition of "fixing the situation" helped him zero in on new ways of making progress that did not require relating directly to his colleague. For example, Dale held meetings even when his colleague declined the invitation to attend. In the past, he would have tried to reschedule the meeting. His new way of operating kept the ball moving down the field instead of wasting time by having to reschedule every meeting she declined.

Perhaps even more important, Dale started to think about his colleague's underhanded techniques to make him look bad as sad instead of as mean spirited and self-serving. He actually began to feel a modicum of compassion for his emotionally challenged colleague. This shift in judgment was just as accurate as his first judgment had been, but it was far more helpful. Now Dale could let go of his disappointment in himself for not being able to relate to this colleague and instead focus on what really mattered: getting the job done and relating to people who could relate: his boss and his employees.

Highly effective leaders often rely on ABT to find third ways out of challenging situations. Ben Stein focused on the profoundly and uniquely positive nature of the debate between President Obama and Mitt Romney. In Dale's case, he regained his reputation as a highly skilled connector by investing in those who could reciprocate in kind. His third way of viewing what it meant to fix this bad situation kept him focused on making progress toward his goals and became his ticket to success.

What You See over Time

Our attitudes toward the time frames of past, present, and future are often unconscious and automatic rather than conscious and intentional. Leaders, like anyone else, can find themselves held back rather than propelled forward by what was, is, or could be. In fact, many leaders I have met seek coaching because they are held back by past mistakes, exhausted by the current pressures they face, or intimidated by an uncertain future that looms too large.

To help you and your team make the most out of the past, present, and future, the next three chapters provide ABT tools on how to shift from held back, exhausted, and intimidated (deficit-based thinking) to heartened, energized, and inspired (asset-based thinking).

2

Focus on the Past

Looking at your professional experiences through the rearview mirror can run the gamut from inspiring to downright depressing—it all depends on the aspects of the past you choose to remember. When you intentionally recall successes, your mood lifts, and you become open to insights on how you were able to achieve your goals. When it comes to remembering failure and setbacks, you can boost your mood and gather insights too, but only if you look beyond the breakdown itself to harvest the lessons and the benefits that are often hidden from plain view.

A positive focus on the past is an indispensable leadership tool. As a leader, you have a major responsibility to give yourself and those you want to influence a positive orientation to the past so that you can learn from it, move faster in the present, and move toward the future you want to create.

In honoring the past for what it can teach, the leader sees a viable path forward. In extracting lessons from past failures, the leader reassures his or her followers that the same mistakes will not be repeated. By standing on the shoulders of past successes, the leader lifts the collective optimism of the team.

It is important to remember that the unwelcome, even disturbing, actions that must be taken for survival's sake often present lessons. At the same time, the circumstances surrounding these actions usually offer rare opportunities to be captured and leveraged. The case that follows is a perfect example of how an economic downturn led to both hard-won lessons and unanticipated gains.

DuPont Company

In 2010, the DuPont Company was continuing its transformation into a market-driven science company. The DuPont Vision was "to be the world's most dynamic science company, creating sustainable solutions essential to a better, safer, and healthier life for people everywhere."[1] The company was also accelerating leadership development by launching a global leadership development program called the Leading Edge with the goal of cultivating resilient and inspirational key leaders.

DuPont's key leaders had their work cut out for them. They were navigating through the aftermath of the global financial crisis, unsure market conditions, and tremendous change. They needed to inspire their organizations to outperform the competition while also delivering outstanding results in terms of innovation, productivity, and company core values like safety.

As one of the faculty in the Leading Edge program, I worked with company leaders to show them how asset-based thinking (ABT) could help them be more resilient and inspiring. One of the first ABT resilience strategies I used was called, "How did we do that?"

I asked participants to recall what happened in late 2008 and 2009 during the global financial crisis, and to assess that time period simultaneously as the "best of times" and the "worst of times." These were the themes that emerged:

It was the worst of times because . . .

"We had to reduce staff."

"We had no idea where the economy was headed and how bad it could get."

"We had no playbook on how to climb out of it."

It was the best of times because . . .

"We stayed true to our core values—no matter what!"

"It was all about what was for the good of the whole."

"We cleaned up and addressed a number of things we never had time to before."

"We got to know our customers better."

"We built even more trust with our teams and with each other."

"We got creative."

This ABT retrospective fortified in the minds of DuPont's key leaders how they and their teams weathered past storms and capitalized on their troubles. I saw leaders in the room move from regret and sadness as they recalled their losses to a real sense of pride as they remembered what they did to survive and even thrive in the face of tremendous past adversity. Their collective memories of what had been gained overshadowed the very real losses that they endured. They left the session heartened and encouraged about their ability to overcome the current economic storm.

We will take a deeper look at the ABT strategies offered to the Leading Edge program later in the chapter. For now, I want you to acknowledge the amazing positive power of recalling times when you and your team were able to move forward in the midst of challenging circumstances. The past is truly a rich treasure trove of fortunate (and unfortunate) situations from which you can learn to lead more effectively.

Gary Spitzer's Story: My Application of ABT

During one session in DuPont's Leading Edge leadership development program, the senior vice president of integrated operations, Gary Spitzer, and I teamed up to tell the story of how he worked with his amazing team to gain community buy-in for a new production facility in the United States. Gary and his team worked arduously to gain the support of reluctant elected officials and other important stakeholders. As he told the story, he highlighted a particular moment during the effort when he applied what he had learned in one of our ABT workshops.

Gary was scheduled to have what he anticipated to be a confrontational telephone conversation with an important stakeholder opposed to the project. Gary's colleague, who already had a relationship with the stakeholder, was not available to sit in on the call and support him. Here is how Gary described his dilemma to the Leading Edge participants:

> I was nervous and unsure how I could have a purposeful call with someone who had opposed us so strongly. I also wished my colleague could have done it instead of leaving it to me! But I also knew this was mine to take on, and I had to get myself in the right mind-set to respectfully engage the other person.
>
> I thought back on my ABT training, and in particular, "Start by giving the person an A," and "assume positive intentions." I had to shift my perspective of the other person. I had to see where we had common and aligned interests. And the more I thought that through, it was the case.
>
> That small shift in perspective allowed me to approach the conversation in the most open, respectful, and constructive way possible. And I am glad to say it was a successful call and important step on the path to finally gaining community support for the facility.

I asked the audience of key leaders to comment on Gary's attitude toward the other person and the inner strengths he drew on to shift his perspective. They pointed out that

Gary showed an attitude of determination and flexibility. Gary himself admitted that he knew he had to find some way of seeing something positive in the person's character or he would have spoken with an unproductive tone and demeanor that surely would have been picked up on the other end of the line. Leveraging his ABT mind-set, he was able to build trust and realize common ground with the key stakeholder.

This part of Gary's story, the self-focused angle, was highly instructive for the audience as well as for Gary. The session participants appreciated that Gary was willing to expose his more vulnerable side ("I was nervous," "I felt alone," and "I was dreading this call"). By letting them in on what he did to manage his mind-set, he became more relatable. Every time Gary told that self-revealing part of the story, his credibility as an executive grew.

For Gary's part, every time he told the story, his own capacity to assume positive intentions increased. Perhaps most important, Gary was able to more clearly see his leadership strong suit as a determined yet flexible thinker. His ABT focus on the past helped him see his competencies as a leader, which made him more likely to leverage them in future endeavors.

A Focus on the Team

To be a leader is to be part of a team. Looking through the lens of collaborative effort can instill in your team a collective sense of confidence that supports your undertakings. Remembering that the contributions of each person ignite in everyone a sense of pride reinforces the notion that the talents and skills of many are necessary to succeed.

Here is a quick yet thorough process designed to help you and others dwell on the details of a collective success. First, work through it yourself; then share the exercise with your team:

Remembering Our Collective Success

- Ask your team to remember a time that they achieved something that at first seemed impossible, a time when the results exceeded expectations. Select one scenario for this reflection exercise.
- Ask members of the team to recall what actions they took. Ask them to describe their thoughts, the effort, the behaviors that drove success. What initial steps did the team take to solve the problem or take advantage of the opportunity?
- Reflect on the positive impact those actions had on you, on others, and on the situation.
- Reflect for a moment on how you and the team felt when you realized beyond a shadow of a doubt that what you were doing was going to work.
- Ask the team to identify the thoughts and behaviors they want to repeat for future situations.

I recommend that you do this type of collective ABT retrospective often with your team. At the beginning of a new project, complete this exercise to energize the group, boost creativity, and instill optimism about future success.

Gary Spitzer's Story: The Genius of Our Team

After recounting what he did to gain support and lay the foundation for the successful operation of the facility, Spitzer elaborated on the efforts of his team on the ground. In particular, he emphasized the work of the scientists who held multiple town meetings, took questions, and patiently shared the facts, data, and science behind the operation. The open and cooperative manner in which the scientists handled themselves ensured those concerned that it was a safe operation that would not have a negative impact on the community or the environment. In fact, it would be good for the society at large.

The audience broke into applause several times as Gary moved from one story to another, painting the picture of the extraordinary efforts taken to secure the necessary support for the new facility.

Another tactic Gary used was providing sensory detail for each story. Sensory detail ignites the imagination of listeners so that they can place themselves into the dynamic of what actually happened (I offer step-by-step guidance on how to stimulate the imaginations of listeners in part 2).

The ABT Rules of Recounting a Past Collective Effort
- Describe the specific behaviors that led to success. Specificity leads to a greater likelihood that the behavior will be repeated.
- Describe the impact of those behaviors on you, the leader. How did they inform your positive impressions of specific individuals and of the team as a whole? When you acknowledge the positive impact, it ignites the reward centers of the

listeners' brains. Again, this leads to a greater likelihood that the behaviors will be repeated.

- Describe the impact of those behaviors on the viability and productivity of the group itself. Acknowledging the collective positive impact keeps the perspective on the team, increasing each person's confidence in fellow team members and in the ability of the team to work together toward success.

A Focus on the Situation

Every situation has something to offer in terms of building momentum and presenting opportunities. Often you may discover that several different aspects of a situation, such as trends, timing, prevailing interests, and attitudes, created an advantageous confluence of forces that propelled your team's efforts forward.

A simple ABT force field analysis is a powerful tool you can use to recall how the situation itself worked for you or against you.

ABT Force Field Analysis

Recall a past situation you faced. Ask yourself and your team:

- What forces were working for us? What helped us build momentum? What conditions advanced our success? Identify five positive, accelerating forces.
- What were the major forces working against us? Identify one or two negative forces.

- What did we do to leverage the accelerating forces? What did we do to eliminate or sidestep the forces working against us?
- Which behaviors do we want to repeat? What knowledge do we want to carry forward? Which situational assets should we attempt to recreate going forward? Which situational pitfalls do we want to stay mindful of?

This ABT force field analysis is a more in-depth version of the "best, worst" retrospective presented at the start of this chapter. Use it to build a clear memory of what you and your team did to make use of positive situational forces and what you did to protect yourselves from negative situational forces. Celebrate your collective and individual skillfulness. Make this memory part of the cultural history that inspires and guides your team.

Gary Spitzer's Story: The Situation Was Our Ally

Gary Spitzer capped off his Leading Edge session by describing how the timing, the circumstances, and the context for building the new facility were favorable for the most part. He highlighted several situational advantages:

- DuPont had a facility that could be adapted to produce the new product.
- DuPont had the scientific data to support the safety of the operation.
- The facility would create jobs.

- Production was part of a technology change toward more sustainable offerings.

Again, I asked the audience to comment on the benefits of hearing this part of Gary's story. Here is what they thought the lessons were:

- It is important to see the opportunity and the objection in the problem so you have a much better starting point for collaboration and mutual gain.
- Collaboration and dialogue to directly address concerns are essential, even with our sharpest critics.
- Don't just sell your position. Listen to all sides and find the common ground.

As you can see, the real situational assets in this situation were easily applicable to a wide array of other situations. Gary's story gave the audience fresh ideas for how to capitalize on similar situations they might encounter in pursuing their own leadership agendas.

What Was My ROI?

Here is one last ABT exercise to help maintain a focus on the positive aspects of the past. Asking yourself the next three questions will illuminate your return on investment (ROI) for a specific initiative or project:

- What did we learn?
- What did we experience?
- What did we achieve?

These questions (and the answers) reflect three distinctly different bottom lines by which you can measure and determine ROI. I first learned of these ROI categories in the research of David McClelland, the late Distinguished Research Professor and Chair of Harvard University's Department of Social Psychology. His work offered empirical proof that motives predict behaviors and results in life for individuals, organizations, and even whole societies. McClelland's work also demonstrated that motives can be taught. For example, he showed in a randomized control group experiment with Indian entrepreneurs that two weeks of achievement motivation training increased their efficacy: their businesses generated 27 percent more jobs and twice the invested capital of individuals in the control group.[2]

It is important for you as a leader to know that you can stimulate different motivational systems from the start to the finish of an important project or initiative. Learning stimulates self-confidence and wards off boredom. Experience is a motivator because most people want enjoyable, enriching experiences, not drudgery. The achievement motive is perhaps the most powerful and rewarding of all. Achieving goals creates a sense of personal competence—what is often referred to as "self-efficacy" or "agency" in psychological terminology. It is empowering to know that through your efforts, you can create the results you strive for, that you are the agent of your own existence.

What Did We Learn?

The answers to this question provide a rich reservoir of lessons that can be applied beginning now. Leaders are much more likely to look for learnings in the wake of failures than they are in the aftermath of successful ventures. This is due in part to the desire to redeem failure in some way. But think about the valuable lessons you can extract out of success stories. Do not overlook or take your successes for granted.

Within seven days of a successful milestone, ask yourself: What did we learn about leading? About teamwork? About our approaches? About our stakeholders? Harvest these learnings so you can keep them top of mind and ready to apply to the next initiative. Create an index in your mind of lessons worth remembering.

What Did We Experience?

This question is almost never considered in an assessment of the past. What did it feel like when you were in the process of pursuing a specific goals? Describe the quality of your experience. Use the following list to help with your reflections on the range of experiences you and your team may have had:

- Rewarding/frustrating
- In sync/out of sync
- Exciting/boring
- Surprising/routine
- In flow/stop and starts
- Out of the box/in the box
- Encouraging/discouraging
- Creative/repetitious

As you think back on the nature of your experience, there will likely be a mixture of positive and negative elements. On balance, however, you will be able to see if it was more on the positive side or vice versa. No one wants to repeat an experience if it was discouraging, repetitious, and boring. By the same token, everyone wants to find ways of duplicating experiences that are encouraging, creative, and rewarding. That is why evaluating the quality of your experiences can be so helpful going forward.

Once you describe the experience, it is a short trip to reflecting on what behaviors and attitudes shaped your experience and made it so positive (or negative). Try to identify significant moments that shaped the emotional valance of the whole experience. Replay what happened in your mind. Determine how you can continue to foster positive experiences and avoid the ones that created a downward spiral of any kind.

What Did We Achieve?

Now come the questions that are most often asked in determining ROI: What were the tangible outcomes? How can we measure success? Having clear metrics to assess results is essential. Common measures include financial gains, market share, customer satisfaction and retention, and employee engagement. Of course, those metrics are best set at the launch of your initiative and tracked throughout its duration so course corrections can be made if you aren't heading in the right direction.

The effective communication of measurable results is what makes them meaningful and rewarding. It is important to note that falling short of the desired metric can be as motivational as exceeding expectations—if you communicate effectively. Even when an effort is falling short, results are best framed positively—for example, "We can catch up," "Let's figure out how . . . ," and "We have what it takes to achieve the goal." When expectations are exceeded, the most powerful question is, "How did we do that?"

From Past to Present

By now you should have a deeper understanding of how to construct positive memories of past events using the Self-Others-Situation framework that can fortify you going forward. By starting with self, you solidify in your mind how you contributed to a success or solution. These memories increase your self-awareness and leadership confidence. They actually create and strengthen neural networks in the reward center of your brain. As these neural networks are strengthened, you can tap into those memories more easily and more intensely in a positive, self-perpetuating cycle.

Creating positive memories around collaborative efforts triggers your appreciation for your team, making it easier to recognize and reinforce the positive behaviors and attitudes of others. By becoming more familiar with your team's competencies and the skill sets of individuals, you can make assignments that better match those competencies. A positive orientation toward the performance of others also creates a reward culture that promotes high performance and aspirations.

By putting the focus on a past situation, you gain insight into how the overall context supported or interfered with your success. Situational analysis is a form of systems thinking, a reminder that you do not ever operate in a vacuum. Every situation has a dynamic set of forces that you as a leader must take into account.

Your memories of creating a vision, solving problems, and seizing opportunities will inform your actions now and in the future and increase your effectiveness—sometimes exponentially. As a case in point, let us take a brief look at a famous historical moment in US history.

On November 19, 1863, President Abraham Lincoln went to the dedication of the National Cemetery in Gettysburg, Pennsylvania. Four and a half months earlier, the Union armies had defeated the Southern forces in the Battle of Gettysburg. Losses on both sides had been staggering.

Lincoln's speech on that hallowed battleground has stood the test of time. The Gettysburg Address continues to be honored and remembered around the world:

Four score and seven years ago, our fathers brought forth on this continent a new nation: conceived in liberty, and dedicated to the proposition that all men are created equal.

Now we are engaged in a great civil war, testing whether that nation, or any nation so conceived and so dedicated, can long endure. We are met on a great battle-field of that war. We have come to dedicate a portion of that field, as a final resting place for those who here gave their lives that that nation might live. It is altogether fitting and proper that we should do this.

But, in a larger sense, we cannot dedicate, we cannot consecrate, we cannot hallow, this ground. The brave men, living and dead, who struggled here, have consecrated it, far above our poor power to add or detract. The world will little note, nor long remember what we say here, but it can never forget what they did here. It is for us the living, rather, to be dedicated here to the unfinished work which they who fought here have thus far so nobly advanced. It is rather for us to be here dedicated to the great task remaining before us, that from these honored dead we take increased devotion to that cause for which they gave the last full measure of devotion, that we here highly resolve that these dead shall not have died in vain, that this nation, under God, shall have a new birth of freedom, and that government of the people, by the people, for the people, shall not perish from the earth.[3]

Notice how Lincoln's opening is a strong reference to times past: "Our fathers brought forth on this continent a new nation." Note how the context framed the challenges and the work to be done under the present dire circumstances: "to be dedicated here to the great task remaining before us . . . that we here highly resolve that these dead shall not have died in vain, that this nation, under God, shall have a new birth of freedom." Lincoln linked that moment of grief and disillusionment to the mighty cause of the nation's inception to boost the spirits and strengthen the resolve of his audience.

When you and your team face daunting challenges that require more gumption than you think you know how to muster, take a lesson from Lincoln. When you find yourself on the brink, fortify yourself by looking to the past for the reasons you set out on that course of action in the first place.

No doubt about it, recalling your past convictions and motives will energize and reinvigorate your actions and feelings about the present moment.

In the next chapter, we examine further how ABT strategies can increase your capacity to see and act on the positive facts and emerging opportunities contained in your set of circumstances. You will learn about leveraging what is happening in the here-and-now to create the best present-moment experiences possible.

3

Focus on the Present

We know that our frame of mind, decisions, and the actions that we take in the present moment set the stage for things to come—sometimes for the better, sometimes for the worse. The quality of our attention, concentration, and creativity in the present dictates the quality of our future. But so often our daily routines are brimming over with meetings, conference calls, and last-minute urgent requests that we do not stop to engage in top-quality thinking in the moment.

Most leaders can barely breathe through the blur of activity, much less reflect on and register the best of what is happening in the present moment. And on the rare occasions when they do step back to assess the situation at hand, they focus on the problems, ignoring the opportunities.

As we discussed in chapter 1, a negativity bias is hardwired into our brains, ensuring that we notice the bad more frequently and intensely than we notice the good. This chapter is about using asset-based thinking (ABT) strategies to reverse that bias and see the positive now. You will practice shifting your attention away from the frenzied moment long enough to spot and leverage the positive facts and dynamics operating just below your conscious awareness.

Kairos Moments and Opportunities

The Greeks have two words for time: *kronos* (or *chronos*) and *kairos*. *Chronos* is chronological, sequential, quantitative time—the time we never have enough of. *Kairos* signifies a time in between, an indeterminate moment when chronological time ceases to be relevant, when something special is occurring, and you are in the zone. Its nature is qualitative; it cannot be measured, only experienced. The word *kairos* translates literally from ancient Greek as the right or opportune or supreme moment.

In Greek mythology, Kairos is the youngest child of Zeus and is the god of opportunity. By suspending your preoccupation with the relentless minute-by-minute march of sequential time (*chronos*), you leave yourself open to the *kairos* opportunities of the present. Being mindful of the positive facts allows you to better see *kairos* opportunities and create *kairos* moments—those moments of clarity, ripe with possibility, when you step outside chronological time and are leveraging the best of yourself, others, and the situation at hand.

Neuropsychologist Rick Hanson calls dwelling on the positive facts happening in the here and now "taking in the good."[1] Hanson suggests that you "take in the good" by intentionally focusing your attention on:

- What makes you feel strong, safe, and capable (focus on self)
- What provides you with deep, meaningful connections to other people (focus on others)
- What gives you a sense of progress or achievement (focus on situation)

By taking in the good using the Self-Others-Situation framework, you imprint a more positive set of assumptions, beliefs, expectations, emotional tendencies, bodily states, and relationship orientations to others into your implicit memory. Your implicit memory system is your experience of the world. By shifting your implicit memory—your understanding of what it's like to be you—in a more positive direction, you will begin to see more of the positive dynamics of the present moment.

Scan-Snap-Savor

Scan-Snap-Savor is a tried-and-true ABT exercise to help you take in the good of a given moment.

Step 1: Scan

Look for the positive facts that are happening in the present or immediate past—something that just happened. You can direct your attention toward any one of the three focus areas: self, others, or situation. The self scan requires you to look for your own leadership strengths, capabilities, efforts, and skills that are showing up in the present moment to move things forward. Scanning others directs your attention toward the behaviors, skills, and contributions that other people are making in the here and now. The situation scan leads you to zero in on the emerging dynamics working in your favor.

Step 2: Snap

Think of "snap" as aiming your mind's camera at a positive fact from your scan and then clicking the shutter to capture it and burn it into your memory. Zero in on just one of the positive facts from your scan in step 1. Create a mind's-eye picture of that fact complete with sensory details of the setting and your state of mind. If you are zeroing in on a positive fact that is based on data or written information, conjure up a representative graphical image or headline. Here are some examples:

- *Self:* "My scan brought up my leadership ability to inspire others. I conjured up a mental picture of myself during our staff meeting announcing a new project we would be undertaking. I could see the chairs around the conference table, the snow on the trees outside of our windows, and the clothing each person was wearing. I could feel the positive buzz of energy in the room as my staff got excited about the project. I could hear their enthusiastic chatter about next steps."
- *Others:* "My scan showed my administrative assistant being extremely helpful and patient with a customer in a protracted telephone call. I closed my eyes and actually saw Colleen sitting at her desk, smiling and chatting away. The room was brightly lit; she had spring flowers on her

credenza. Her voice was calm, her manner respectful, and her body language engaging."

- *Situation:* "My scan brought up the number of followers we have managed to collect on Facebook. I saw the number at the top of our Facebook fan page on my computer monitor. I pictured a frequency polygon with a steep upward trending red curve that mapped our increase in followers from 213 just three weeks ago to over 6,000 today. I tracked the positive trends in our Google Analytics reports and saw the inspiring comments from fans on our Facebook wall."

Step 3: Savor

Once you have snapped that image of a positive, present-moment fact, it is time to turn it into a lasting positive experience. Dwell on that image and relive your internal experience of the moment. How do you feel? Grateful? Enthusiastic? Optimistic? Resourceful? Spend thirty to sixty seconds cherishing the positive emotions associated with that positive fact.

Let the full measure of the experience sink deeply into your implicit memory. Savor it. In less than ninety seconds, you have allowed yourself to step outside the hustle and bustle of the day. You have experienced a brief but energetic pause that recharges you and helps you to shift the way you look at yourself, others, and the situation at hand in a more positive direction.

Use Scan-Snap-Savor whenever you need a brief respite from the unrelenting hurry and pressure of chronological time. It is a highly effective way to intentionally put your focus on the positive facts of the present. By momentarily transcending the tyranny of chronological time, you are refreshed and energized—primed to see and seize the opportunities right in front of you.

Seizing the *Kairos* Opportunity

Now that you are open to seeing the best of what's happening in the present moment, it is time to take action. *Kairos* opportunities require swift and decisive action to be realized into *kairos* moments. In *Kaironomia: On the Will-to-Invent*, Charles White defines the *kairos* opportunity as "an opening . . . or, more precisely, a long tunnel-like aperture through which the archer's arrow has to pass." He writes that successful passage requires that "the archer's arrow be fired not only accurately but with enough power for it to penetrate."[2]

We have all encountered *kairos* opportunities when we had to respond swiftly and accurately else forgo success—for example:

- Focusing on the trajectory of the ball and swinging the bat at just the right moment in just the right way to make a home run
- Noticing a lull in the conversation and using the opening to say just the right thing that propels the team to action
- Listening between the lines of what is being said to sense the deep-seated desire and fulfilling it

These are everyday acts of transcending ordinary time and entering into the *kairos* zone of opportunity.

The ability to see and seize *kairos* opportunities, moments ripe with possibility, is critical to becoming a more effective and magnetic leader. Recently a client recounted a story about her father that underscored the importance of being vigilant and primed for decisive action.

The father of Louisa Jaffe, chief executive officer of project management company TAPE, was raised during the Great Depression and had to draw on great entrepreneurial creativity to help support his family. In Georgia, when he was about three years old, his grandmother sent him and the rest of the grandchildren to a cotton farm to pick bales for a penny each.

There was a special prize for picking the most bales that day—$100, a huge amount at that time. An elderly man who was determined to win the prize picked 100 bales, leading him to a decisive victory. Louisa's father had picked just one bale of cotton and the experience left the industrious youngster with the determination to do better. By his actions, the elderly man had taught him that it takes more than just opportunity to make things happen; it also takes focus, vision, and hard work, a lesson he never forgot in his eighty-one years of life. The little boy grew up to become an Army Air Corps officer who directed the loading of the atom bomb into the *Enola Gay*, a feat that required innovation because it had never been done before. Later, he became a serial entrepreneur and inspired his daughter to take the risks required to start up a government contracting business, something Louisa and her husband had to be able to envision and reach for even before it existed.

Reflect for a moment on the lesson from Louisa's father: it takes focus, vision, hard work, and opportunity to be successful. Think of *kairos* opportunities as emerging positive dynamics, fluid sets of positive forces that may be converging. Applying focus, vision, and hard work to realize the potential of the *kairos* opportunity is what will make you a successful leader.

Kairos moments happen when action and opportunity intersect (figure 3.1). Consider these examples of *kairos* opportunities and how they can be turned into *kairos* moments:

Opportunity: I sense the potential client is more interested in our services than ever before.

Action: I spend more time listening and conversing with her, deepening our bond.

Moment: The potential client and I experience a connection that transcends the sales transaction. We are both energized by our rapport and eager to further our business relationship. The potential client agrees to become an actual client.

Opportunity: I sense the high degree of energy, focus, and collaboration of my team on this project.

Action: I acknowledge their efforts and success and ask them to apply their skills to solving a different, thorny problem.

Moment: Primed by their past success and energized by the acknowledgment of their strengths, they work enthusiastically and collaboratively to come up with new, innovative solutions.

In these examples, the leader senses the presence of the *kairos* opportunity—one that can change the course of what is happening for the better. He or she fires the arrow of action

Figure 3.1 How to Leverage the Best of the Present

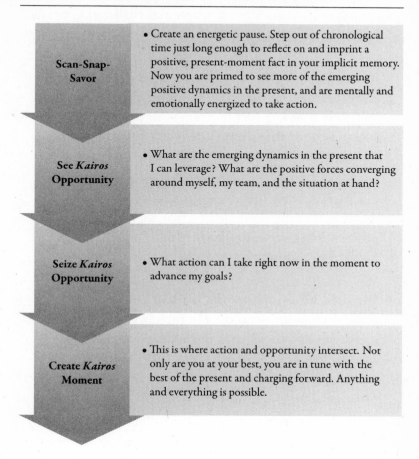

Scan-Snap-Savor	• Create an energetic pause. Step out of chronological time just long enough to reflect on and imprint a positive, present-moment fact in your implicit memory. Now you are primed to see more of the emerging positive dynamics in the present, and are mentally and emotionally energized to take action.
See *Kairos* Opportunity	• What are the emerging dynamics in the present that I can leverage? What are the positive forces converging around myself, my team, and the situation at hand?
Seize *Kairos* Opportunity	• What action can I take right now in the moment to advance my goals?
Create *Kairos* Moment	• This is where action and opportunity intersect. Not only are you at your best, you are in tune with the best of the present and charging forward. Anything and everything is possible.

accurately and with power, seizing the opportunity and creating a *kairos* moment.[3]

Seizing Opportunity from Negative Dynamics

New learnings and opportunities can be culled just as easily from negative dynamics. Using ABT strategies, TAPE CEO

Louisa Jaffe became adept at seeing and seizing the *kairos* opportunities hidden within negative and challenging circumstances. Here is her story:

> After much hard work, we won a contract with the army, beating out the much more experienced incumbent. At our first meeting with the primary coordinator of the contract, he said, "I'm not happy that you won the contract and I think you'll lose it."
>
> We knew we faced some very challenging barriers, but we also knew our strengths. Our asset-based thinking training reminded us that we had to keep a positive focus, so we smiled and told him, "We look forward to shifting the way you look at us."
>
> We took his negative opinion as a challenge, but we also used it to shift how we saw and leveraged the present-moment situation. He told us we were too inexperienced, so we used our inexperience as an asset to lower the former contractor's guard and create a dynamic where he and his team did not feel threatened by us.
>
> We took the army coordinator's skepticism of our abilities and used it as opportunity to strengthen our resilience. We created opportunities to learn and build relationships. We exceeded expectations by focusing on the emerging dynamics—positive and negative—of the present and milking them for everything they were worth.

Louisa milked the present moment by scanning for every opportunity to learn and grow; she did not limit her focus to the objectively positive dynamics. Next, when she saw an opportunity, she zeroed in on it. Finally, she fully engaged with the opportunity, acting swiftly and decisively to leverage her assets, those of the other players (including the naysayers), and those of the situation. She fired the arrow of action accurately and with enough power to penetrate, ensuring her success.

Louisa's mantra has become, "Where is the asset here?" It keeps her focused on the present and what it has to offer. By maintaining this vigilant focus on seeing and seizing *kairos* opportunities, she intentionally creates *kairos* moments for her team, her clients, and her business.

From Present to Future

When you have a compelling vision of the future, the present moment is alive with opportunity and possibility. You are energized by the knowledge that what you do today is contributing to tomorrow and the months and years ahead. You are actively shaping your career, your team, your organization, your whole life, because you have a vision in mind. Your outlook on the future is your capstone leadership perspective. Conversely, without a clear vision of the future you want to create, the present loses its meaning.

In a very real sense, these chapters on the past and present have been building toward the next one on the future. Now it's time to hone in on how ABT can give wings to what has already happened and what is happening right now.

4

Focus on the Future

When a leader can see beyond the present to a future worth marching into, it is like a beacon lighting the way and pulling everyone involved forward. You can actually feel the momentum when even a relatively small step is taken toward achieving that future. In this dynamic, the pursuit becomes a gift not a grind.

Your ability to see a rewarding future is what leadership researchers Bernard Bass and Antonakis Avolio refer to as a "strong force of leadership."[1] This is because a rewarding vision motivates both leaders and followers to perform to their full potential. The science backs this up. The reward pathways in the brain use the neurotransmitter dopamine to motivate and reward desire-driven behavior. Studies have shown that dopamine is released when there is a stimulus worth working hard for.[2] A rewarding vision ripe with opportunities to be pounced on provides such stimuli, acting as a strong motivator.

A Moderate Focus on the Future

The ideal time orientation is an intense focus on the positives of the past and a moderate focus on the positives in the present and future. According to renowned psychology professor Phillip Zimbardo, a moderate future orientation gives you the wings and freedom to fly while ensuring that you do not miss out on the opportunities of the present.[3] His research showed that living too much in the future can put you at risk for burnout because you deny yourself the energy that comes from focusing on and celebrating past and present-moment victories. The asset-based thinking (ABT) framework is aligned with Zimbardo's advocated time orientations, ensuring that you are leveraging the most out of your past, present, and future.

Envisioning a Positive Future

I often encourage the leaders I work with to apply the Self-Others-Situation framework to envision a rewarding future. You can conjure up your vision by entering any one of those three doors first. For instance, many visions of a rewarding future start with the leader seeing a solution or opportunity (a situation) that will make a significant positive difference to his or her products, services, customers, and organization. Alternately, a leader may start the visionary process by identifying a new or hidden team capability or desire (others). Finally, your positive vision of the future could begin with you (self). You could be imagining the skills you will develop next or the new subject matter you want to master.

Your own personal aspirations as a leader are a legitimate place to start the visioning process. When you start imagining a positive future for yourself, you can rest assured you will be personally committed to achieving the rewarding outcomes. But the main point here is that no matter where you start—self, others, or situation—you will also need to consider the other two parts of the framework to empower and complete your vision. Consider the examples below.

A Self-Oriented Start to a Positive Future

Recently Robert, a smart and successful chief financial officer (CFO) for a top-tier pharmaceutical company, came to me for executive coaching. His initial struggle was with his temper, but as we progressed, his end goal became developing his mentoring skills. Seeing himself as a strong mentor was the starting place for his vision of a rewarding future. However, Robert needed to include the facets of others and situational circumstances to power-up his vision to the fullest extent.

When Robert first came to me, he was in hot water with the chief executive officer (CEO) and other members of the executive leadership team. He was an exemplary CFO in every respect, but one: he had a volatile temper and was prone to berating his team whenever anyone made a mistake.

Robert was aware of this shortcoming and was actually contrite and apologetic after each outburst. He just had no idea when his meltdowns would come on and did not know how to prevent them. Robert knew his job was on the line if he could not get his disruptive behavior under control.

I worked with Robert to identify his hot buttons. The general trigger pattern that emerged was his surprise at the careless mistakes of others, accompanied by the belief that he was the only one smart enough to correct the problem. Robert's work involved shifting from deficit-based thinking to ABT whenever a challenging situation that fit the general trigger pattern occurred. With this goal in mind, Robert began using some of the ABT tools from chapter 1: the see-think-feel awareness tool and the ASA (acknowledge-scan-shift) shift. Robert first applied the see-think-feel awareness tool to identify and label his negative emotions:

"I *see* the careless mistake."

"I *think*, 'How stupid can you be?'"

"I *feel* backed into a corner and hopping mad."

By identifying the see-think-feel sequence and labeling his feelings, Robert gained new insight. He realized he would have more control over his actions if he could apply the see-think-feel awareness tool in the heat of the moment. Then, by using the ASA shift tool, he was able to:

Acknowledge the triggers for his negative emotions (careless mistakes)

Scan for the potential benefits or gains from addressing the problem (the creation of teachable moments)

Act by taking a positive step toward realizing that benefit (ask his team members to work with him to figure out how the mistake was made and what could be done to better in the future)

Robert rehearsed these ABT strategies daily on his commute to work. Essentially he was retraining his reaction to mistakes that had not yet been made, but could easily happen given the junior level of financial experience and acumen of his team. The mental rehearsal did not prevent the mistakes, of course, but practicing see-think-feel and the ASA shift did change Robert's perspective and behavior; it prepared him to respond constructively when mistakes were made.

As Robert's orientation toward his staff became more positive, his see-think-feel sequence also shifted:

"I *see* a mistake."

"I *think*, 'We need to fix that.'"

"I *feel* curious and eager to solve the problem."

Robert's junior staff noticed the dramatic change in their boss and began to see him as a collaborative mentor. Robert himself realized how much he enjoyed teaching others and the great value that could come from imparting his knowledge and experience to his staff.

Through this process, Robert created a positive vision of the future that began with his becoming a first-rate mentor— the self component. Then Robert and I made sure that we expanded his vision to include others by determining how his team members could benefit from the mentoring process in terms of skills, confidence, and teamwork. Finally, he looked at the business situation to identify the value of his ability to delegate responsibilities to his newly empowered team.

Think about the progression of this coaching engagement:

- Robert was at risk of losing his job due to disruptive, demeaning outbursts.
- He used ABT strategies to control and eliminate subsequent outbursts.
- He began to see his own potential as a mentor.
- He created a Self-Others-Situation vision that fully outlined the rewarding future that becoming a great mentor would provide for himself, his team, and the business as a whole.

Who Is on Your Mount Rushmore?

Robert pursued his vision of becoming a mentor in many ways. One of the most powerful strategies he used was asking himself, "Who is on my Mount Rushmore?" Mount Rushmore celebrates America's greatest leaders. Carved into the face of the mountain in Keystone, South Dakota, are the heads of four outstanding US presidents: George Washington, Thomas Jefferson, Theodore Roosevelt, and Abraham Lincoln.

The question, "Who is on my Mount Rushmore?" requires you to consider four people you admire and why. Who would you put on your own personal Mount Rushmore? The second part of this exercise is contacting those four people and asking them how they do what they do.

I have witnessed this exercise help many leaders achieve a personal aspiration, for example, developing strategic thinking or conflict resolution skills or developing patience. Robert is one of them.

I asked Robert, "When it comes to first-rate mentors, whom do you admire? Who would be on your Mount Rushmore?" He identified a peer who led the sales team for the company, one who had led the effort to establish a mentoring program in a professional association to which he belonged, his son's baseball coach, and his business school graduate advisor.

Before Robert interviewed those four people he admired for their mentoring skills, I reminded him of the following ABT principle: what you see and admire in someone else, you already have in yourself. Otherwise you wouldn't see it. This is what is known as the positive projection dynamic. It is a sibling in psychology to the negative projection dynamic that most people are familiar with: "It takes one to know one!" We are attracted to certain positive qualities in others because we possess those qualities ourselves in some measure—even if only a glimmer of them. This principle is worth remembering; it helped to show Robert which of the seeds of being a great mentor he already possessed.

The vice president of sales told Robert he always made the effort to see multiple potentials in a mentee. He then asked the person which potential he wanted to cultivate. The leader of the mentoring program told Robert that matching the mentor with the mentee's career aspirations was fundamental to his success. His son's baseball coach confided that giving positive feedback relative to strengths and effort was key.

Finally, Robert's graduate advisor believed in asking his students over and over, "What do you want, and why is it important to you?"

These nuggets of wisdom allowed Robert to see that he did have a strong foundation for becoming a first-rate mentor. He could apply the same tactics as his Mount Rushmore four to develop his mentoring skills. This insight made it possible for Robert to create his own set of positive expectations around achieving his vision. And as we know, positive expectations are essential to achieving any type of personal development goal.

Robert formulated the positive expectations for his own mentoring success by generating five answers to the following stem sentence: "I will become a first-rate mentor because . . ." Here are his answers:

1. "I have had great mentors myself to show me the way."
2. "I am a good listener, and I want to become more patient."
3. "I am able to give positive feedback."
4. "I can see what will help my team members be successful in their careers."
5. "I get satisfaction from watching others succeed."

Robert wrote down these positive expectations and kept them in full view as he pursued his vision. In less than a year, the concern about his outbursts had evaporated, and he became a well-known and well-respected mentor in his company (self). In fact, other leaders now came to Robert for guidance on how to mentor. His team became more proficient and now operated as trusted advisors to the regional business teams (others).

Finally, Robert could focus on developing the company by acquisitions (situation).

Many leaders would benefit from creating a rewarding vision of the future that starts with self. It may seem counter-intuitive at first, but think about Robert's story. His vision of becoming a highly effective mentor led to team proficiencies and empowerment, as well as tangible business growth.

What is it that you want to develop in yourself? How could you grow as a leader? What do you want to learn? These questions are well worth the reflection and the pursuit. As you grow, others will benefit, and situations will improve. Try it. Your personal aspirations could be the start of a bright new vision not only for yourself but also for your team and your organization.

An Other-Oriented Start to a Positive Future

Gwen, the newly hired chief information officer at a large company, said to me one day, "I have to get my team to be more strategic. Each person works hard and is a good contributor, but no one knows the strategy well enough to prioritize activities and make the tough trade-off decisions."

Gwen had been in her new job as chief information officer for less than ninety days when she spotted a major barrier to her success: "I am the one making all the strategic moves. They feel micromanaged, I feel exhausted, and we are behind on making our key performance indicators." Gwen was hitting a wall. She knew she needed to develop a positive vision of the future for her team, or the problem would continue to undermine their collective success.

The first order of business for her was to imagine what her team would be thinking and doing differently if they were truly strategic. But instead of relying on her own vision, we decided she would go to her team for input. She took the pulse of the team first to bring their aspirations and needs to the surface. She went on a mission to learn as much as possible about the future the team most desired.

Reflect for a moment on what it means to set your sights on a vision that fulfills a need rather than creates a new demand. Initially Gwen's vision for her team was that they become more strategic so they could prioritize better and make better trade-off decisions. When she queried her team about they wanted to happen, she realized that there was distinct overlap between her and their visions. By taking the collaborative approach and hooking her vision to their aspirations, she was able to fulfill their needs and hers without having to impose her will on them. Whereas a top-down, create-demand approach may have alienated her staff and bred resentment, her collaborative approach engendered goodwill and a collective enthusiasm toward achieving the new, shared vision.

Of course, there are other times when a top-down, create-demand approach is necessary and welcome. That is what I refer to as leading by lightning (versus leading by listening). I discuss the merits of both leadership styles at the end of this chapter.

What Do You Need? What Do You Want?

Gwen set up interviews with each member of her department to determine their aspirations for themselves and for the team as a whole. Here were her findings:

"We need to better understand what the company as a whole wants from information technology so we can prioritize the requests we get."

"We need cross-training so we can backfill for one another when there are high-priority, urgent assignments that need more resources."

"We need to know what Gwen is saying to and hearing from the CEO and his leadership team."

"We want to be more collaborative."

"We want to be able to say no to low-priority requests."

"We want to stop, recognize, and celebrate when we make progress."

"We want more feedback from Gwen about how we are doing."

Initially Gwen was calling the shots about how her team needed to improve: "I need to get my team to be more strategic." She was creating what felt like a new demand and imposing it on her team. However, with her interview findings in hand, Gwen could engage the team in fulfilling their own needs and wants: there was automatic buy-in since there was no imposing necessary.

As Gwen and I reflected on the team's assessment, we identified ways in which she could lead more effectively. Gwen began communicating the conversations she was having with senior leaders more often and more substantially. She also acknowledged the role her feedback could play in taking her team to the next level. Finally, it was clear to Gwen that collectively fulfilling her team's need and wants could reap great benefits for the company, and her own vision would be achieved. Top-priority cybersecurity requests would take precedent over other less mission-critical information technology requests. In addition, her team would be better able to say no to lower-priority requests without ruffling feathers because they could explain why another project needed to come first.

By collaborating with her team to develop a vision for the future, she made a solid start. But when we included Gwen's own perspective, we took that vision to the next level. She imagined a future in which she would have the time to focus on assessing technology trends and building relationships with her high-level internal customers. Then Gwen envisioned her company shifting from a cybersecurity vulnerable to a cybersecurity safe (situation). This complete vision of a positive future motivated Gwen and her team to work diligently and tirelessly to make it a reality.

Gwen's case serves as a good reminder of the need for you as a leader to take the pulse of what your team wants to happen before setting a vision. Once you have assessed their needs and wants, you can hook your vision to their aspirations. In effect, the group's desires become part of the mosaic for your vision of the most rewarding future.

A Situation-Oriented Start to a New Future

Visions that start with the situation fall into two camps: solving problems and seizing opportunities. Solving problems often leads to a vision ripe with new opportunities to be seized. This is what happened to Ena Shelley, dean of the College of Education at Butler University in Indiana.

Scheduling and space issues at Butler were leading to overbooked classrooms and students unable to sign up for the courses they needed to graduate. After months of failed attempts to solve the problem, Ena Shelley asked her fellow deans, "What would this problem look like if it were solved?" The conversations that followed led to a collaborative resolution of the nagging systemwide problem.

Building on that success, Ena and her faculty in the College of Education created a new vision filled with innovations regarding how they could use time and space and build better learning relationships with their students. Ena took charge of the situation, turning the problem into a vision for a better future. Her leadership helped her colleagues to include themselves in this new vision. And once Ena was able to link her own aspirations as a leader to the new vision, her own leadership skills and ability to inspire others grew exponentially.

Imagine this: You are running a university with six colleges. Students are unable to sign up for the classes they need because too many are being scheduled simultaneously. To make matters worse, larger classes have no space to meet. In short, the operations of the university are teetering on the brink of mass confusion. This was Dean Ena Shelley's reality.

Previous efforts to solve the problem had failed miserably. Ena explained, "It was a silo approach that kept backfiring. There was no communication between colleges and departments, so we kept pushing the responsibility to fix the situation back down into the silos." After four rounds of getting nowhere, Ena had the idea of asking her peers to shift from a problem-focus to a solution focus. At the beginning of the fifth meeting of the deans, she attempted to break through the impasse by asking, "What would the problem look like if it were solved?" Here is her recollection of what happened next:

> The room was silent. People did a double-take. Then, slowly but surely, a process of discovery began. Our group had a vision of students being able to sign up for the classes they needed. Each class had the appropriate teaching space. Faculty were satisfied with their schedules, and students were able to graduate on time.
>
> One person suggested that we think about teaching in spaces that are not traditional classrooms. Another person asked, "How many large spaces do we actually have on campus?" We started identifying seminal questions and learning from each other for the first time since the problem arose. That was when we decided to invite others from each silo (registrar's office, curriculum scheduling committee, etc.) into the conversation. Prior to this, we had reports, but no live input from and interaction with the key committee members.
>
> The direct conversations with other knowledgeable people led to looking across the silos to see the big picture, as well as a vision for our preferred future. People stopped judging and blaming one another and started collaborating in creative ways.

As a result of this solution-focused process, Ena said, the deans became much more aware of each other's issues: "We have established a much deeper level of trust with each other." This team of leaders is now tackling five-year visions that will transform the way we teach and learn.

Positive Provocations

Ena used another ABT tool to develop, with her faculty, a five-year vision for the department. By using positive provocations, she encouraged new ways of looking at situations in order to generate new strategies.

Positive provocations usually begin, "I wonder what would happen if . . ." and call for a positive answer to the question. For example, Ena asked her faculty, "I wonder what would happen if we saw our students as highly competent and as capable as they really are." In this case, Ena's positive provocation led the faculty to embrace the learning innovation known as flip classroom in which students are viewed as teachers as well as learners.

Ena's positive provocation planted the seed and gave her faculty the permission to create their own innovative visions. This ABT tool was key in helping them to develop their capacities for seeing a positive future. In this way, Ena fulfilled the other component of the new vision.

Ena's focus on the self component of the new vision involved seeing herself as a more patient leader who gives her staff the time and space to pursue new innovations. As she works toward that vision, she constantly asks herself, "Do I push, nudge, inspire, or wait?" So far, she has learned that it is often best to wait and let things happen: "I live in the silence. I float for a while until I am able to see what is ready to happen.

Then I say something that leans in the direction of what others are saying and feeling."

Leadership by Lightning or Listening

Ena's self-focused vision zeroed in on a leadership style that many would do well to develop. I call it leading by listening. This style is in contrast to leading by lightning. To lead well you need to master both.

When you lead by listening, you wait, watch, and listen deeply, looking for patterns of ideas. Then, at just the right moment, you speak up, inviting others to see what the future could be from their point of view. When this style works, people are grateful and inspired. The leader has said what they were thinking the whole time. They feel strong ownership and are ready to do whatever it takes to achieve their vision.

Leading by lightning relies on leader-driven ideas. When using this style, the leader has a big idea. He or she rides in on a white horse (metaphorically), announcing to the team: "How about THIS!" When this style works, people are also grateful and inspired. The leader has saved the day. The heavens have opened up, and lightning has struck to reveal a brand new future.

It is important to keep in mind that leaders need to be flexible and competent at both approaches. Part of being effective as a leader is knowing which approach is appropriate for the situation and the audience—and for your own leadership style.

In general, leaders use leading by lightning to convince others to adopt, invest, and sanction their visions. It requires stronger advocacy. Advocacy skills include the ability to clearly state your position (vision), explain your thinking, give examples, seek others' points of view, encourage challenges, and call others to action. This leadership style works best when there are no common patterns around the desires of the team and people are at a loss for what needs to happen next.

Leading by listening, which usually warrants keen inquiry skills, empowers others to create their own vision. Inquiry skills include the ability to conduct probing interviews, gather diverse perspectives, and see patterns and themes in needs and aspirations. This leadership style works best when there is overlap among the desires of the team.

Gwen shifted from a leadership by lightning mentality to leadership by listening. She had her own vision imperative that her team become more strategic. Then she interviewed each team member to surface the themes and patterns in the team's thinking about what would move their culture and their performance to the next level. She realized that leadership by listening was the appropriate approach in this situation and worked to enunciate a shared vision that incorporated her own ideas as well as those that of her team.

As we move to part 2 in this book, "What Highly Effective Leaders Say," you will learn just how important developing your advocacy and inquiry skills are to being an effective leader.

Sometimes "say" means to advocate for the way things have been, are, or need to be in the future. At other times, it's about inquiring into how others view the past, present, and future. Both skill sets are driven by your commitment to involve and enroll others. As we move forward in our framework, you will learn how what highly effective leaders see can and should inform what they say. This is where it gets even more interesting.

PART 2

What Highly Effective Leaders Say

Speak to the mind, heart, and spirit

5

From See to Say

Toddlers remind us that what we say is a direct expression of what we see and feel. They first speak to acknowledge what they see. They proudly point to an object and speak its name: mama, dada, dog, moon. They also speak to express their needs and wants: toy, milk, mama, and so on.

Take the word *mama*. With just a small shift in inflection, "mama" can go from an acknowledgment to a full-blown expression of desire: MAH-MAH! Speaking with such strong desire gets attention and evokes swift action. In this case, on hearing the clarion call, the mother acts swiftly to embrace her child.

Now imagine a toddler sees a stranger appear. She feels frightened and cries out: MAH-MAH! Fear creates an unmistakable quality in the spoken word. The cry puts mom on high alert. She acts swiftly to hold her child, this time, to assuage fear.

The simple language of toddlers highlights the intimate relationship between sight and speech. Our ability to take visual sensory input and then represent it in the spoken word is the first loop in a complex, interdependent system. Once we see something, we begin investing meaning into it. Over time, we develop a set of assumptions and beliefs about it, drawing on our experiences and how it made us feel. This is how we form the perceptual sets I mentioned in chapter 1. But the see-say system is a self-reinforcing process that functions in either direction: as language and implicit memory develop, what we say also influences what we selectively see.

These toddler examples also emphasize how what we say is laced with our emotions and values—whether we consciously divulge them or not. Small children hardly ever attempt to hide their feelings or biases. What children say communicates their true intentions and feelings, sometimes to a fault. Perhaps it is this simple, direct, and honest speech that draws people to children.

As adults, we come up with all kinds of reasons to cloak our feelings and dress up our motives to be more socially acceptable. Maybe we don't want to show negative emotions for fear of upsetting someone. Often we attempt to speak without emotion to portray ourselves as calm and rational. But I promise you: your speech will always reveal what you see and, as a consequence, what you want, what you fear, and what you value. No matter how hard you try to disguise or dress it up, what you say will uncover what you see.

We should make it our job as adults—and especially as leaders—to be as congruent as children. If we are fearful and would rather come off to others as courageous, then we should shift how we are viewing the circumstance, changing what we see to match what we want to say. Speaking with courage, hope, and authenticity are the marks of effective leadership, and they are possible only if we focus more of our attention and effort on our assets than our deficits. This is the essence of the asset-based thinking (ABT) approach to leadership.

Saying It with Substance, Sizzle, and Soul

There are three assets you can leverage when you speak: substance, sizzle, and soul. Each is important and distinct enough to call out as a separate element, but in reality, they overlap and reinforce each other.

Substance refers to the content of what you say. To be authentic, leaders must ensure that they are knowledgeable about and comfortable with the content of their messages. While this may seem obvious, all too often leaders speak from scripts and slideshow decks into which they had little or no input. It is obvious when this occurs, and it radically short-changes the speaker's impact. No matter how accurate or elegant your talking points may be, you must engage with the material and make it your own before you say it.

Substance is your credibility card, whether you are speaking to one person or a thousand. Saying it with substance convinces your listeners that you know what you are talking about. Now more than ever before, people have access to a world of information. You can and will be fact-checked, perhaps even as you are speaking. People will choose to listen to you based on how much substance they think you have. Your perceived mastery of the subject helps them decide how open they are to what you are saying. Think of it as the intelligence quotient of what you say.

Sizzle is the color and detail of what you say. It is about using your words and your voice to evoke emotion in your listeners. It is a true, heartfelt expression of the feelings—your feelings—about your message. Consider these two versions of the same story:

> The queen died, and then the king died.
>
> The queen died, and then the king died *of a broken heart.*

While the first version fulfills the substance requirement, the second, which adds the sizzling detail of how the king died, provides insight into the relationship between the king and queen. This emotional insight helps us to form a deeper connection with the story, making it more meaningful and memorable. Including emotional detail in the communication piques our imagination, and we become invested in the unfolding story and the storyteller. It makes us want to hear more.

Think of sizzle as the emotional quotient of what you say. Daniel Goleman, psychologist, noted author, and frequent contributor to the *Wall Street Journal*, identified emotional intelligence as a major contributor to leadership effectiveness and success in other aspects of life.[1] Having an awareness of your true emotions and choosing the right words and tone to express them will draw people in and make what you say more engaging and, ultimately, more memorable.

The *soul* of what you say refers to the why—why the message is so important to your listeners, your mission, and you. Most leaders shortchange soul. They assume that the why of their message is self-evident and does not need to be stated explicitly. Nothing could be further from the truth.

People long for a deep, abiding sense of purpose. They are inspired to be part of something bigger than themselves, something more important than growing market share or increasing company profit. Increasing market share and profit are important, of course, but they do not inspire. Having a meaningful *why* does.

Think of the soul of what you say as your meaning quotient. People follow people, not just great ideas. When you say it with soul, you embody your idea. People see that you mean what you say and that what you say is meaningful. Since 2006, Indra Nooyi, PepsiCo's chief executive officer, has been focused on transforming the huge corporation from a "North American fun-for-you company" to one that lives up to the mantra, "Performance with Purpose."[2] "It doesn't mean subtracting from the bottom line," she explained in a 2007 speech, but rather "that we bring together what is good for business with what is good for the world."[3] To fulfill this vision, she has been investing in the development of healthier snacks, campaigning against obesity, and reducing the company's reliance on fossil fuels in favor of renewable energy.

Nooyi's unrelenting and long-term mission to balance profit with social responsibility is the kind of mighty cause that inspires. For her vocal and soulful commitment to this mission, *U.S. News & World Report* named her one of America's best leaders in 2008.[4] As I was writing this chapter, PepsiCo's 2012 fourth-quarter earnings were released showing that Nooyi's efforts were finally beginning to pay off in terms of the bottom line.[5]

Soul elevates what you to say to a meaningful plane. When you give voice to your highest values and beliefs, you lead your followers to trust you and believe what you want to happen is important. You help them to identify with you as someone they want to make a meaningful difference with.

What You Say and How You Say It

What you say has high impact when listeners:

- Remember your message beyond the conversation or presentation
- Have a change of heart brought about by the message
- Take action as a result
- Influence others to join forces with you

For truly high-impact communication, you must take into consideration the substance, sizzle, and soul not only of your words but also of your delivery.[6] To be an effective leader, what you say and how you say it must be aligned. In the next three chapters, we explore substance, sizzle, and soul in terms of both content and delivery to ensure you make the maximum impact on your followers. But first, take a look at table 5.1, which provides a road map for developing a speech and presenting it the ABT way.

The Substance-Sizzle-Soul Connection

In summary, substance is the foundation of the communication—the what. It must be present. It determines whether the

Table 5.1 The Lead Positive Communication Road Map

	What You Say	How You Say It
Substance	What must be accomplished: • The case for change • The positive vision of the future What I want to make you, the listener, understand What the benefits will be for: • Followers • The organization • The community, industry, the world	Authoritatively Confidently Convincingly Clearly Rationally
Sizzle	How we will get there: • The strategy • The road map • The story How we will work together to: • Forge alliances • Neutralize opposition • Recognize contributions • Overcome obstacles • Solicit help and guidance • Navigate ups and downs	Passionately Empathetically Invitingly Energetically Openly
Soul	Why this is important to: • The bigger picture • Our values and beliefs • Our organization Why this is so important: • To me (my skin in the game) • To my commitment • For you to be involved	Sincerely Vulnerably Inspirationally Congruently Inspiringly

audience listens at all. Without it, sizzle and soul are superfluous. However, substance rarely inspires, and that is where sizzle and soul come into play. Sizzle is the engagement factor. It is how you say what you say and how you make the listener feel. Sizzle ignites listeners' imagination and draws them into the story. Soul provides the meaning factor. It points to why what you are saying is important and why you believe in your message.

One last word before we dive into the depths of substance, sizzle, and soul: in essence, saying is a form of doing. In fact, in linguistics and in the philosophy of language, "speech act" refers to persuading, convincing, enlightening, inspiring, or otherwise getting someone to do or realize something. Your speech acts can also commit you to a future course of action.

What you say prepares you and the people you lead for what you need to do, for walking the talk. And ultimately what you do creates the results you seek. We will explore in depth what highly effective leaders do in part 3. For now, take this intermediate step in maximizing your leadership effectiveness. Over the next three chapters, you will learn more about the ABT strategies for saying what you see with substance, sizzle, and soul.

6

Say It with Substance

On June 18, 1940, Winston Churchill gave a speech to the British House of Commons that was instrumental in turning the tide of World War II. The British were seemingly deflated on every front, but Churchill believed he could change the course of the war by laying out the facts of the situation and his solution to the problem with conviction. Here is an excerpt from that great speech, "Their Finest Hour":[1]

> What General Weygand called the Battle of France is over. I expect that the Battle of Britain is about to begin. Upon this battle depends the survival of Christian civilization. Upon it depends our own British life, and the long continuity of our institutions and our Empire. The whole fury and might of the enemy must very soon be turned on us.

Hitler knows that he will have to break us in this Island or lose the war. If we can stand up to him, all Europe may be free and the life of the world may move forward into broad, sunlit uplands. But if we fail, then the whole world, including the United States, including all that we have known and cared for, will sink into the abyss of a new Dark Age made more sinister, and perhaps more protracted, by the lights of perverted science.

Let us therefore brace ourselves to our duties, and so bear ourselves that if the British Empire and its Commonwealth last for a thousand years, men will say, "This was their finest hour."

Churchill made his case for change clear. He lay out a positive vision for the future. He explained why it is important and what was needed from his audience to make it happen. His sentences are filled with concrete facts but also include sensory detail and analogy. His images are compelling, his verbs bold and authoritative. For most people, reading this passage is inspiring; it instills hope.

I encourage you to listen to a recording of Churchill delivering this speech (search online for "Winston Churchill, speeches, audio finest hour").[2] What does his voice telegraph to you? I hear solemnity, gravity, and earnest resolve. I also hear confidence and conviction. Most important, the substance of his delivery matches the substance of his words. This cohesion between the message and the messenger is what draws us in, invites our full attention, and provides credibility. Churchill reminds us that saying it with substance is a function of what we say and how we say it. As a leader you must be substantive and have substantive ideas. The result is that when you speak, people know that you have done your homework. Your wisdom shines through loud and clear.

In this brief yet poignant portion of this speech, Churchill applies asset-based thinking (ABT) to frame a positive image of what must be discussed, decided, and done:

> "What General Weygand called the Battle of France is over." (past)
>
> "I expect that the Battle of Britain is about to begin." (present and future)
>
> "Let us therefore brace ourselves to our duties, and so bear ourselves . . ." (present)
>
> "If the British Empire, and its commonwealth, last for a thousand years, men will say, 'This was their finest hour.'" (future)

Using the assets of logic and conviction to weave these three time frames provides listeners with a strong sense of continuity and the historical significance of the moment. This is another important reminder: in establishing their case for change, leaders need to say what they see as the assets of the past, present, and future if they want listeners to fully appreciate their role and contribution. This positive context shows people how much their efforts truly matter to achieving the positive vision of the future.

Although I chose this excerpt from Churchill's speech as a prime example of saying it with substance, it also reveals how Churchill tapped into the elements of sizzle and soul. As I mentioned in the previous chapter, the assets of substance, sizzle, and soul almost always overlap to contribute to the overall impact of what a leader has to say.

Churchill's *substance* as a leader is fully present in the very words he uttered. Reading his speech leaves no doubt to the importance and credibility of his ideas. Furthermore, Churchill's dedication to these ideas is communicated in his delivery. Next, by his use of sensory detail and imagery, he reinforces the significance of his message and his willingness to lead. This is the *sizzle* factor at work, drawing the listener in emotionally. And when it comes to saying it with *soul*, Churchill focused on the bigger picture at hand, just how much was at stake for him personally, and for the world at large: human freedom. This mighty cause uplifted the spirits of his listeners, making the sacrificial efforts to come worthwhile.

Practice, Practice, Practice

So what does Winston Churchill, one of the greatest wartime leaders in history, have to do with you? You probably don't lead a nation, and your stakes are not nearly as high as the protection of human freedom at all costs. Nevertheless, don't discount the link between you and this highly effective leader. You have more in common than you might think.

Regardless of your leadership domain and innate talents, saying it with substance takes practice. You may have heard that it takes over ten thousand hours of practice to master a skill. Journalist Malcolm Gladwell revealed this research finding in his 2011 best-seller, *Outliers: The Story of Success.*[3] I believe this is great news for all leaders who aspire to be highly effective communicators. It means that when it comes to saying it with substance, sizzle, and soul, practice will get you there.

Churchill placed great importance on preparing and rehearsing his leadership messages. In his classic treatise *On Leadership*, noted political, education, and military leader John W. Gardner wrote:

> Communication is, of course, the prime instrument of the leader/motivator, and all leaders take their communicating seriously . . . Churchill spent a good part of his life rehearsing impromptu speeches. One day his valet, having drawn his master's bath shortly before, heard Churchill's voice booming out from the bathroom. The valet stuck his head in to find out of anything was needed. Churchill, immersed in the bathtub, said, "I was not speaking to you, Norman, I was addressing the House of Commons.[4]

Of course, the substance of what you say as a leader is relative. But whether you are fighting for human freedom or rallying your team behind a new corporate initiative, the leadership principle remains the same: highly effective communication takes practice, practice, practice.

Janice's Story

Janice is a client of mine who runs a small technology and social media consulting company with her tech-savvy husband, Jim. Janice saw herself as the business leader of their small firm. Jim saw himself as the technology lead. As part of their business strategy, Jim was responsible for writing an e-book guide for parents searching for the best, most affordable colleges for their high school children. Their strategic plan called for the book to be published in the August-September time frame and marketed to parents whose children needed to apply for college in the following fall and spring semesters.

Jim did not finish the e-book as scheduled, and Janice was highly irritated. She felt let down and was worried about the lost revenue for their business. She also felt guilty that she had not been paying attention to his progress, or lack thereof, and regretted not stepping up to help.

As the CEO, Janice decided to take the lead and speak with Jim about how to salvage the situation. First, she used ABT to shift how she saw the missed deadline. Instead of dwelling on the missteps, Janice identified three upsides of moving the deadline to the following spring. She decided to make those upsides the centerpiece—the substance—of her message. Next, we worked together on how she could deliver the message substantively in a way that laid out the problem and solutions in a credible and motivating manner.

She outlined what must be accomplished: "Jim, you and I both believe that publishing and marketing the e-book will bring us revenue and establish us as trusted advisors for parents and high-schoolers searching for the right college."

She focused on a positive vision for the future and the benefits for their business and target audience: "The delay has set us back, but it also has hidden benefits. If we publish the e-book next May, we can market it as a graduation gift for sophomores and juniors. If parents buy the book in May, they will have more time in the summer to get started planning with their teens. Plus, the extra six months will give us time to edit and upgrade the content and get testimonials that will help sell the book."

As Janice crafted the substance of her message to Jim, I could see her energy and excitement grow. She rehearsed the delivery with me several times to get a sense of how she would sound to Jim. She practiced to ensure her confidence in the solution shone through in her words. As I listened to her, her confidence was contagious.

Jim agreed immediately. Janice's use of the assets of logic and passion to frame a positive image of what must be done showed Jim that she had done her homework and that she had utmost confidence in this new vision for the future. It was obvious how much Janice believed in him and how much she valued the project as a way to develop their business. In a significant way, Janice took the lead by seeing and saying the substance of the path forward. This was Janice's "finest hour" speech.

Substance as Your Credibility Card

As a leader, you can use your credibility as an asset to move your team forward. The strong substance of your words and your delivery can create a magnetic pull that draws listeners in. People want to achieve, they want their efforts to count toward something important, and they want to join forces with a leader who they believe in.

Say It with Substance Self-Tests

These say-it-with-substance self-tests are designed to reveal strengths and areas for improvement in crafting a credible message and delivering your message with confidence.

Rate yourself on the assessments in tables 6.1 and 6.2 using this five-point scale: 5 = Excellent, 4 = Very Good, 3 = Average, 2 = Needs Improvement, 1 = Novice.

For any item you gave yourself a 4 or 5, mark those as your strong suits. For any item you gave yourself a 3, 2, or 1, mark those as areas for improvement. Then select and concentrate on one area for improvement from each assessment: content and delivery. Remember that the content assessment items primarily target how you craft the content of your message, and the delivery assessment items focus on how you show up when you present your message.

You can also use the self-tests as a checklist when preparing content and rehearsing the delivery of a presentation, speech, or even a more informal conversation. The checklist approach helps you remember to give special attention to the areas you want to improve.

How to Say It with Substance

Using the now-familiar ABT Self-Others-Situation framework, let us continue our discussion on how to craft a substantive leadership message.

Self

Identify what you want to contribute to the substance of your message. One great way to do this is to go back to the idea of

Table 6.1 Lead Positive Substance Content Assessment

When I speak, I . . .	Excellent	Very Good	Average	Needs Improvement	Novice
Demonstrate deep subject matter expertise and an experience base in what I want to accomplish.	5	4	3	2	1
Create a vision that speaks to the case for change.	5	4	3	2	1
Give the general nature of what could be possible in the positive future.	5	4	3	2	1
Outline my call to action enough so people know how to advance, how to lean forward into the future.	5	4	3	2	1
Articulate the benefits of achieving the vision for all key stakeholders.	5	4	3	2	1

Table 6.2 Lead Positive Substance Delivery Assessment

When I speak, I . . .	Excellent	Very Good	Average	Needs Improvement	Novice
Feel free enough to say whatever it takes for the message to catch fire.	5	4	3	2	1
Use my energy as the driving force for the message.	5	4	3	2	1
Use confidence and humility in key moments.	5	4	3	2	1
Show conviction so others are convinced that it is possible to make a positive difference no matter how challenging the circumstances.	5	4	3	2	1
Am fully committed to my audience.	5	4	3	2	1
Make eye contact with my listeners.	5	4	3	2	1

committing speech acts as a leader. Ask yourself: What do I want to accomplish with this message?

Substance-Oriented Speech Acts

Inform	Enlighten
Recall	Convince
Signify	Envision
Reinforce	Remember
Reveal	

As you craft your message, ensure that the substance reflects the goal of your speech act. Think of speech acts as clarifying your role in delivering your message. Substance-oriented speech acts give you a strong platform and frame your point of view. The speech act you select helps you create a through-line for what you want to make the listener understand.

Others

What do you want from those who are listening to your message? Always be sure you have a clear call to action—even if the action is a change of heart or shift in attitude rather than an actual step to be taken. One good way to establish your call to action is to fill in this sentence: "As a result of hearing my message, I want you, my listeners, to . . ."

Substance-Oriented Call to Actions
   Open your minds to a new possibility.
   Change your assumptions.
   Realize there is more than meets the eye.
   Forgive and forget.

Get onboard.

Give this idea a chance.

Consider this solution.

Tell other people.

Take this action now.

Try this step.

Make a commitment.

The call to action is one of the most overlooked aspects of saying it with substance, yet it is vital to your leadership effectiveness. Providing a clear call to action gives your listeners something to do. You want an active audience, not a passive one. You want your listeners to own your substance as if it were their substance. That's what a clear call to action can do.

Situation

The situation framework helps you communicate the context, timing, urgency, and feasibility of your message. Think of it as your case for change.

Remember the lines in Churchill's speech that framed the situation in June of 1940: "What General Weygand called the Battle of France is over. I expect the Battle of Britain is about to begin. Upon this battle depends the survival of Christian civilization."

Also recall how Janice laid out the situation for Jim: "The delay has set us back, but it also has hidden benefits."

These are great examples of how important establishing the overall context and case for change of your message can be. You don't need to speak volumes to describe the situation. Say just enough to ensure your call to action and positive vision for the future make sense in the minds of your listeners.

Substance in Action

Recently I worked with the chief executive team of St. Andrew's Resources for Seniors System, which provides a range of services to seniors, such as affordable retirement housing, in-home health care, assisted living, and skilled nursing. Along with other business leaders, St. Andrew's CEO, Mary Alice Ryan, COO, Diane Meatheany, and CFO, Greg Elliott, attended a Lead Positive program put on by The Cramer Institute. Their goal was to find ways to make St. Andrew's more financially secure and establish the company as a regional leader in senior services. They needed help creating a vision that they could communicate to their employees to get their buy-in. I worked with the three-person team to create a substantive vision message using the framework from chapter 5:

What Must Be Accomplished
- Case for change
  - Health care reimbursements and regulations are changing constantly. We don't have the stability of the past. The present and the future are uncertain and volatile. We must become a stronger, more viable, and more visibly effective organization to survive and thrive.
- Positive vision of the future
  - St. Andrew's as an industry leader and the number one senior services company in the region.

What We Want to Make You Understand
- We have a strategy for making this vision a reality with your help.

What We Want You to Do (Call to Action)
- Open your mind and hearts to this challenge.
- Give us your feedback on what it will take to become number one.

What the Benefits Will Be
- For leaders and employees
  - Acquire new skills in teamwork and leadership
  - Be more engaged and empowered
  - Job security
- For the organization
  - Creation of a more sustainable and strategic organization
  - Increased ability to attract funding from grants and philanthropic donations
- For customers
  - St. Andrew's seniors and their families will feel more secure in the quality of their care.

The leadership team knew that this first draft of their vision message would change and improve as they practiced how to *say* it and as they involved others in shaping the vision and strategies going forward. Our initial work together involved rehearsing how each person would deliver the message. I asked them to express the *substance* using their own words and styles. This meant each came up with his or her own outline with different examples and different ways of expressing their own commitment to the cause.

Next, they practiced delivering the substance to each other and to a small group of other participants in the Lead Positive program. I asked each of the three leaders to deliver one thought to one person at a time. This strategy helped the speaker gain the confidence to look people directly in the eye and speak at a pace listeners can absorb. We also practiced standing still and projecting their voices so that it was easy for listeners to hear.

When it came to speaking style, Greg was naturally reserved but charming, Diane was forceful and funny, and Mary Alice was gracious and reassuring. All three styles were effective. I coached each person to connect to the type of energy each felt when he or she was being clear, authoritative, convincing, and strong—that is, their personal substantive style. They practiced delivering their versions of the message using their own styles.

Hearing the unique and powerful deliveries of the vision from each of the St. Andrew's leaders was an amazing experience. As they heard each other communicating the vision, each in her or his own respective styles, their confidence in the feasibility and wisdom of their vision grew. They also came to respect and value each other's substantive styles. This process laid a strong foundation for how they could extend their impact by adding and emphasizing the elements of sizzle and soul.

In the next chapter, we discover how these three leaders (and other exemplary role models) made their messages sizzle in the imagination of their listeners. You will learn how to say it with sizzle using metaphors, analogies, and stories so rich with sensory detail that they come alive in the minds and hearts of your listeners. You will also learn how to embody the energy of empathy and form deep, lasting connections with your stakeholders through your words and your delivery.

7

Say It with Sizzle

While the substance of what you say may be your credibility card, it is the sizzle of your words that makes them stick. When you say it with sizzle, you are engaging the hearts and minds of your audience, inviting them to feel and invest in your message. In short, the sizzle is your leadership story.

I have been researching the motivational value of saying it with sizzle for the past twenty years. One of the major tools I've found is telling rich stories of lessons learned, defeats suffered, and victories won. I was fortunate enough to witness the power of strong storytelling when DuPont's senior vice president of integrated operations, Gary Spitzer, whom we first met in chapter 2, used the story of Secretariat winning the 1973 Belmont Stakes horse race during his keynote address at a major internal conference.

After Gary presented his vision for the operations arm of DuPont, he asked, "What will it look and feel like when we get there?" He then told the story of how much he was affected as a child watching Secretariat win the Belmont Stakes by thirty-one lengths and, with that win, the Triple Crown, the highest accomplishment for a thoroughbred racehorse. In Gary's view, it was one of the greatest athletic achievements in history by one of the greatest thoroughbreds of all time. Gary then showed a video of the race.[1]

When the video ended, Gary told the audience how the video still brings tears to his eyes (it did that day as well). He showed a picture of himself with Secretariat taken in 1988. Gary just had to go visit him. He quoted from the official notes of the Chart Caller for the *Daily Racing Form*, the horse-racing publication of record, from that race day: "All that power. All that balance. All that heart. All that speed. Secretariat was ready to roll. And the margin kept widening, and widening, and widening."[2]

Gary explained that when Secretariat passed away and the autopsy was performed, they found that his heart was more than twice the size of the average equine heart. The veterinarian was amazed at how "perfect" it was and surmised that it was the secret to Secretariat's speed and success.[3] That was Gary's vision for the organization, he continued: "A strong, powerful organization that will win with a margin that kept widening and widening. An organization with the heart of a champion, with the heart to win and the heart for each other and for our customers."

After the conference, Gary told me he had never had so many people thank him for his message about putting heart into your work. I was not surprised in the least, because what Gary did in his opening remarks was filled with spellbinding sizzle. Let us review what happened:

- Gary showed the Belmont Stakes race on a big screen to capture the audience's attention and imagination.
- The audience felt the growing excitement as they watched the race unfold. (I suggest you watch this race for yourself so you too can experience the thrill it engenders.)
- While the audience was still feeling the excitement of victory, Gary made his point about how heart can be the engine of accomplishment.

Gary's leadership message left an indelible mark in the memories of the conferees, thanks to the unforgettable experience they had reliving Secretariat's victory. The story of Secretariat became the story the audience wanted to experience for themselves. They wanted to strive for victory, have the heart of a champion, and "win by thirty-one lengths."

A story well told transports listeners to a different time, place, and plane. It captivates emotions and provides an exciting trajectory of experiences full of hope, struggle, uncertainty, and surprise. Stories show us how to live life. Stories help us lead.

The Hero's Journey

As you pursue your goals and vision, you will harvest innumerable real-life leadership stories that you can use to keep your followers engaged and motivated. However, there is one type of story I want to share with you, as I believe it is seminal to your leadership effectiveness: your Hero's Journey.

Leadership stories have been told for centuries in the form of heroic myths and legends. When well-known mythology professor Joseph Campbell conducted comparative research on those timeless stories, he found similar themes and patterns that he characterized as the Hero's Journey.[4] I have taken these themes and turned them into a crafting tool to help you create your own Hero's Journey, the powerful leadership story of what lies ahead in the pursuit of your goals.

Your own journey is the story of the future you seek come true. You must craft it as if you believe it and tell it as if you have already lived it. Through telling your Hero's Journey, you address your own experience as a leader. You articulate the path forward complete with plausible windfalls and challenges encountered along the way to victory. You detail the experiences of others—your allies, enemies, mentors, and detractors. You describe hurdles so high and barriers so solid that only creativity and determination can prevail.

Step 1: The Call

Campbell's research reveals that at the outset of any heroic adventure, the Hero (or the leader) is presented with a challenge or opportunity that opens up a whole new world. The "Call" is so named because this step is about pursuing a vocation—something you were born to do, your mighty cause.

Remember that you are casting yourself in the role of Hero in this adventure story not because you are self-centered or suffer from hubris. Rather, you are the protagonist, the leader who is instigating the journey, the one with the vision.

Others will surely contribute, and some will be essential to the quest, but you are the one who hears the Call first.

Remember as well to consider each step through the lens of our Self-Others-Situation framework. But as you begin to craft and tell this seminal story, you need to put yourself front and center. It is you, the leader, who is ultimately responsible for how things turn out. This is your story. There will be plenty of room for others and for situations as the story unfolds.

Use the following reflection questions to help you articulate your role and your Call as the hero of your story:

- How did I come to realize the need for change?
- How do I know that I am no longer willing to accept things as they are?
- How do I know beyond a shadow of a doubt I believe in this effort and this cause?

Step 2: The Resistance

Every hero fights resistance of some kind. Campbell reminds us that the Hero often balks at the threshold of adventure because he or she is facing the greatest of all fears: fear of the unknown. Usually at this point the Hero encounters a mentor or sage who offers advice and encouragement. The mentor often knows the Hero is ready before the Hero does.

For this step in articulating your story, ask yourself reflection questions such as these:

- How come I am fearful or hesitant about pursuing this leadership journey?

- How will I overcome my fears and hesitancies?
- How have people guided and encouraged me to take this on?
- How do I know that I am ready?

Step 3: The Threshold Crossing

Once committed, the Hero moves from the way things are toward the way things can be. The new reality is palpable. There is no turning back. As you consider this part of your Hero's Journey, reflect on these questions:

- How has our work environment been holding others back, blocking their vision?
- How can I entice people to cross the threshold to beyond business as usual?
- How can I demonstrate my commitment and resolve?

Step 4: The Journey

As the Hero proceeds toward answering the Call, the journey is filled with windfalls and blessings, tests and challenges, allies and enemies. Some are predictable; most are not. Ask yourself:

- How can I describe the forces working for and against my success? Remember the asset-based thinking (ABT) five-to-one principle: consider five positive forces for every negative one.

- How can I honor and work with allies?
- How can I foster resilience in myself and others?
- How can I cultivate enough optimism and confidence to move ahead?

Step 5: The Supreme Ordeal

One of the most consistent findings in Joseph Campbell's research is that every hero encounters a profoundly dark moment, a time when he or she is at risk of losing everything. In literature this moment is often called the nadir, the lowest point.

It is extremely valuable to your team and other stakeholders to hear you speak about the potentially dire circumstances that could lie ahead and how they will be handled. You can describe similar past challenges you have faced and how you overcame them.

In this step, highlight how you tap into your strengths to overcome the Supreme Ordeal: the point in your leadership story when you show that you are truly the Hero, that you have what it takes and that we have what it takes to win against all odds. Consider these questions:

- How will we prevail against significant resistance and barriers?
- How have we demonstrated resolve in similarly challenging circumstances?
- How will we find the strength and determination to stay the course?

Step 6: The Return Home

Having survived the darkest hour, the Hero takes possession of the treasure and returns home with boons and elixirs from the adventure. As Campbell illuminates, the Hero returns to the ordinary world with unexpected and timeless lessons that transform the human experience for the better.

As you set your sights on the most important benefits of making your vision come true, ask yourself:

- How will this experience change me, others, and the situation for the better?
- How will posterity remember us?
- How will we have fulfilled our destiny?

You may have noticed that for each of the steps, the reflection questions begin with the word *how*. I have structured the questions this way for two important reasons. First, saying it with sizzle is about the how—how you describe how to get there and how you and your team will work together. The how questions help you to dive into the sizzle and articulate at a high level what to expect from the journey—how it will feel, how it will unfold, and how it will be possible.

The second reason for the how questions is to make it easier for you to feel and speak with emotion as you chronicle your Hero's Journey. Your emotion is the essence of how you say it with sizzle—passionately, empathetically, invitingly, energetically, and openly. Your emotion is what moves and touches listeners. They will feel what you feel. And when your team and other stakeholders are emotionally drawn to you and your cause, they will get on board and be happy they did.

An ABT Leader with Sizzle

In summer 2012, I spoke at a government contractor conference in Washington, DC. I attended a keynote address given by Ted Leonsis, vice chairman emeritus of AOL and a well-respected business leader and social entrepreneur. I was looking forward to hearing him speak on innovation, technology trends, and leadership, but instead, I was treated to a seventy-five-minute speech on the role of happiness in business.

Leonsis began by telling his story of personal reckoning. At age twenty-six, after selling his first business for $22 million, he had "arrived." He described himself as "satisfied, but not particularly happy." And then one day, he got on the wrong plane.

Leonsis spoke in detail about his harrowing experience of being a passenger on a disabled plane trying to land. First, they jettisoned fuel. Next, there was twenty-five minutes of controlled terror as they moved the passengers around the cabin for balance. Finally, they proceeded to land the plane without landing gear. During the frightening chaos, Leonsis made a bargain with God: he asked God to save him in return for spending the rest of his life giving back.

Leonsis lived, and he stuck to his bargain. On the day I heard him speak, some thirty years after the miraculous crash landing, Leonsis was still giving back. His keynote message was about approaching happiness like a business: establish a vision, develop plans, and be systematic about setting and achieving happiness goals.

Leonsis pointed to a study that concluded that for those who reported they were happy all or most of the time:[5]

- 90 percent could list their life goals
- Almost 100 percent cited a community of interest (that is, a community of people who share a common interest or passion)
- 75 percent had three or more communities of interest
- 60 percent had three or more outlets for self-expression
- 80 percent reflected on gratitude regularly or daily
- 70 percent actively engaged in charitable giving
- 73 percent believed they had a higher calling

Leonsis threaded the rest of his speech with advice tied to the research findings about how to live a happy life all or most of the time. But the reason those of us in the audience remembered and were inspired to act on Leonsis's advice was because of his personal reckoning (the sizzle), not his statistics (the substance). Whenever you can add a relevant, personal story to your commentary, that story is what will make your substance stick. Sizzle, through story and other devices, makes the audience identify with you. It opens them to hearing the substance of what you have to say.

Say It with Sizzle Self-Tests

As a leader, you want to engage people's emotions and imaginations. You want to take them out of their day-to-day experience and transport them to a place and time where they can think new thoughts, have new experiences, and break through to new and better ways of living and working. This is what you make possible when you say it with sizzle.

The say-it-with-sizzle self-tests are designed to reveal your strengths and areas for improvement when it comes to crafting a memorable message and delivering it in ways that motivate and inspire.

Rate yourself on the two assessments in tables 7.1 and 7.2 using a five-point scale: 5 = Excellent, 4 = Very Good, 3 = Average, 2 = Needs Improvement, 1 = Novice.

To calculate your assessment results, for any item you gave yourself a 4 or 5, mark those as your strong suits. For any item you gave yourself a 3, 2, or 1, mark those as areas for improvement. Select and concentrate on one area for improvement from each assessment: content and delivery. Remember that the content assessment items primarily target how you craft your message, and the delivery assessment items focus on how you show up when you present your message.

You can also use these self-tests as a checklist when preparing content and rehearsing the delivery of a presentation, speech, or even a more informal conversation. The checklist approach helps you remember to give special attention to the areas you want to improve.

How to Say It with Sizzle

Using the now-familiar ABT Self-Others-Situation framework, we'll explore how to incorporate yourself, others, and the situation into a leadership message that sizzles.

Self

Identify what you want to be memorable and motivational in your message. One effective way to do this is to go back to the

Table 7.1 Lead Positive Sizzle Content Assessment

When I speak, I . . .	Excellent	Very Good	Average	Needs Improvement	Novice
Paint a clear and compelling story of how we will meet challenges and win the victory.	5	4	3	2	1
Identify my role and how I intend to lead.	5	4	3	2	1
Recognize the talents and strengths of my team and other key stakeholders.	5	4	3	2	1
Invite people to get on board and make valuable contributions.	5	4	3	2	1
Emphasize that building strong relationships is as important as achieving results.	5	4	3	2	1

Table 7.2 Lead Positive Sizzle Delivery Assessment

When I speak, I . . .	Excellent	Very Good	Average	Needs Improvement	Novice
Use mood to heighten listeners' emotions and inspire them to get involved.	5	4	3	2	1
Pick up on social cues and the emotional state of my audience and tailor my message accordingly.	5	4	3	2	1
Engage and interact with my audience so they feel involved.	5	4	3	2	1
Show my own positive emotions so others will feel what I feel.	5	4	3	2	1
Encourage humor, enthusiasm, and empathy.	5	4	3	2	1

idea of committing speech acts as a leader. Ask yourself: What do I want to accomplish with this message?

Sizzle-Oriented Speech Acts
- Invite
- Empathize
- Apologize
- Celebrate
- Encourage
- Empower
- Support
- Enroll
- Connect

Find ways of incorporating speech acts into your message. Remember that speech acts can clarify your role as leader. They help to establish your relationship with your audience and evoke emotions. The speech act you select helps you create a through-line for what you want to make the listener feel.

Others

What emotional response do you want from those listening to your message? With regard to substance, I asked you to be sure of your call to action. When it comes to sizzle, be sure to have a clear invitation to feel. You may want to evoke differ-ent emotions at various junctures in the delivery of your message. Make notes about which emotion you want to invite and when.

Sizzle-Oriented Invitations to Feel
- Uplifted
- Enthusiastic
- Curious
- Decisive
- Courageous
- Safe
- Relieved
- Strong
- Honored
- Respected
- Worthwhile

Your invitation to feel will evoke emotions from you as well as from your listeners. What you feel, they will feel too. Emotions are contagious, so you must be fully emotionally engaged in what you are saying.

For many leaders, public displays of emotion feel taboo. Of course, I am not advocating letting your emotions run away with you. No one likes to see a leader who is emotionally distraught or out of control. But people do like to gauge a leader's emotional quotient—what gives each of us depth and make us real, accessible, likable.

You can learn to be more emotional and therefore more engaging and motivational when you speak. One way is by reading aloud segments of effective leadership speeches with compelling emotional tones.

One of my personal favorites is Ronald Reagan's "Tear Down This Wall" speech from June 12, 1987, in which he challenged Soviet Union leader Mikhail Gorbachev to destroy the Berlin Wall.[6] I often coach leaders on how to be more emotionally intelligent by practicing the following excerpt aloud. Listen to the original speech yourself, and then try saying it aloud. Keep practicing until you feel that you can match Reagan's emotional tenor:

> Are these the beginnings of profound changes in the Soviet state? Or are they token gestures, intended to raise false hopes in the West, or to strengthen the Soviet system without changing it?
>
> We welcome change and openness; for we believe that freedom and security go together, that the advance of human liberty can only strengthen the cause of world peace. There is one sign the Soviets can make that would be unmistakable, that would advance dramatically the cause of freedom and peace.
>
> General Secretary Gorbachev, if you seek peace, if you seek prosperity for the Soviet Union and Eastern Europe, if you seek liberalization: Come here to this gate! Mr. Gorbachev, open this gate! Mr. Gorbachev, tear down this wall![7]

Situation

The situation framework helps you determine how best to engage your listeners at a particular moment in time. Knowing your audience's frame of mind—uncertain or clear, hesitant or ready, worried or excited, or in the dark or knowledgeable—is essential to selecting the right stories and engagement strategies. The sizzle of your message must serve the needs of your audience: their interests, concerns, aspirations, and well-being must be your paramount focus. You, your emotional tone, the stories you tell, and the images you paint must connect with your listeners' most ardent hopes and desires.

I had been working with a CEO and his five-person leadership team for the past year to assist them in planning a successful divestiture process. Two weeks before the closing date of the sale, the team needed to announce the sale to employees, customers, suppliers, and the community at large. Because these stakeholder groups were not privy to the earlier phases of the process, the announcement was going to come as a surprise.

In preparing their announcement remarks, the leaders took into account the unique interests and concerns of each stakeholder group relative to the sale announcement. They brainstormed on what the sale would mean from the unique perspectives of each constituency, profiling the likely hopes and fears of each. Painting the picture of how each group would react to the sale made it possible for the leaders to customize stories and create talking points that would best satisfy the interests and concerns of each group.

Most important, the CEO and his team had to come to grips with the fact that because they were well past their own initial anxieties and concerns, they needed to tap into two essential virtues: empathy and patience. To demonstrate empathy, each leader (including the CEO) crafted a personal story of how he or she initially reacted to the uncertainties associated with the divestiture process. Each story also revealed what it took for them to come to terms with their worries.

The chief operating officer spoke of her anxieties about losing her organization's well-earned reputation for putting safety first. She knew safety would always be a personal value for her, but she wondered if the new company would champion safety as emphatically as her previous company did.

The head of sales and marketing had been worried about finding a buyer with a solid customer base and a reputation for being customer focused. If customer relations with the new company were not as strong, he wondered what could be done to rectify that situation. How fast could the turnaround happen? His concerns multiplied as he visualized the worst-case scenarios.

As each member of the leadership team made his or her respective announcement of the sale of the company, each told personal stories of shifting from concern and worry over potential problems to curiosity and enthusiasm over what possibilities the sale might spark. They offered to give time and support to everyone else now needing to shift from negative apprehension to positive engagement.

Engaging in tailored preparation enabled the leadership team to speak directly to the specific fears, hopes, and desires of each key stakeholder group: employees, customers, suppliers, and community. Divulging their personal stories of struggle allowed the people within each group to sense their leaders' positive intentions and authentic efforts to walk in their shoes, and this promoted mutual trust. Trust was the essential ingredient for moving forward together in executing the subsequent phases of the divestiture process.

Scholars have written volumes on knowing your audience's story and anticipating how your audience will react to a new story. I find *The Secret Language of Leadership* by noted management scholar Stephen Denning particularly enlightening when it comes to mastering the fundamentals of meeting an audience where they are.[8] I highly recommend this book for extended story-crafting guidance.

Sizzle in Action

As the leadership team from St. Andrew's Resources for Seniors System, whom we met in the previous chapter, moved beyond the "what" of their shared vision to become more financially secure and establish the company as a regional leader in senior service, each created notes on the "how" narrative.

Diane Meatheany, chief operating officer, went first. She used the Hero's Journey to expand and enrich the story of how St. Andrew's would move forward and how she would show up as a leader. As you review the notes she made, think about your own agenda and how you would answer the reflection questions.

Step 1: The Call

As you read Diane's reflection on the Call, you will get to know her better. She is revealing her personal take on and stake in the effort as she lays out the plan to shift from operating in silos to cross-functional teams. You can see, even from these brief initial notes, that Diane is crafting the color commentary that will make her conversations and presentations more interesting and more memorable:

How did I come to realize the need for change? I would say I have been aware of our need to restructure and reorganize for more than ten years! At first, it was just a hunch. For the past two years, I have felt we have to change. It's not a choice anymore; it's an imperative.

How do I know I am no longer willing to accept things as they are? I am pulled in so many different directions that I am not serving anyone well. I know I need to delegate the day-to-day and be more strategic. It's been hard to give up staying close to the action.

How do I know that beyond a shadow of a doubt I believe in this effort and this cause? Ever since we made the commitment to our new vision, I feel the excitement I felt when I first started at St. Andrew's almost twenty years ago. I know that the leadership team is determined enough and creative enough to crack the code on how to eliminate the silos and replace them with the team-based matrix organization we need.

Step 2: The Resistance

Diane's emotions range from excitement and enthusiasm to appreciation and a bit of apprehension here. If you are like most other leaders, you too will experience a wide range of emotions, especially at the beginning of a significant change effort. The ABT principle here is that being aware of your emotions and using them to guide what you say will make your message resonate. Emotional tone is something people listen for. It gives them a reason to trust that you are vitally committed to the cause:

How do I know I am fearful or hesitant about pursuing this leadership journey? When I try to visualize how the employees will respond to this new way of working together, I see a lot of confusion and complaining. I am nervous about exactly how to frame the effort.

How will I successfully overcome my fears and hesitancies? I've decided to try out my communication talking points with a small group who can give me feedback on which messages will be most motivational. They will be a big help in making the first few meetings I have a success. This will set the stage for embracing the change as we move through the more complicated steps.

How have people guided and encouraged me to take this on? Both Mary Alice (CEO) and Greg (CFO) have independently confided in me that I have the most heavy lifting to do in achieving our shared vision. They have confidence in my ability to garner support from the leaders of each function and each entity. They know I will be collaborative in how I approach creating the strategies and implementation plan. I so appreciate that I have such clear support.

How do I know I am ready? This new effort is all I think about morning, noon, and night. I can't wait to get started!

Step 3: The Threshold Crossing

In this step, Diane is beginning to focus on others—the people she depends on to make things happen in real time. You can think of this step as the time to enroll others to lead the charge with you:

> *How has the current work environment been holding others back?* Everyone is so busy, working like crazy to meet deadlines and objectives, that they don't have time to think or reflect. They are operating out of the status quo. It is our job as their leaders to start the conversation about what can be done differently and better.
>
> *How can I entice people to cross the threshold beyond business as usual?* I need to carve out the time, the place, and the process. If I do that, they will respond.
>
> *How can I demonstrate my commitment and resolve?* I can start by hosting and designing a series of retreats that involve cross-functional groups who can internalize the vision together and start collaborating on strategies. I can ask them to own the process.

Step 4: The Journey

As Diane makes notes about the Journey, she has a focus on the situation. This will be your natural emphasis as you consider what is working for you and against you. It is difficult to predict the exact forces you will face, but like Diane, you can anticipate how you might deal with the most likely challenges:

> *How can I describe the forces working for and against us?* The positive forces propelling us forward are many. For example, the baby boomers are aging and living

longer and healthier lives. They expect to be respected and to receive the support and services they desire. In turn, their children want the best for their aging parents and will select a provider who best meets their parents' needs. Furthermore, most of our employees are truly dedicated to serving the elderly. Taking our services from good to great will appeal to their sense of mission. Finally, there is so much uncertainty in the health care reimbursement system, this could be our chance to set the standards in our field. With all that said, I want us to remember that our habits and fears of losing power may hold us back. I truly believe that our greatest chance for sabotage resides in our own minds and hearts. We will have to work hard to keep our eyes on the vision, so we can achieve the changes in attitudes and behaviors that will drive our transformation.

How can I honor and work with allies? I will acknowledge those who get onboard quickly and show enthusiasm for the vision from the start. I will select those individuals to lead the strategy teams. They will become the real champions. I will do whatever I can to recognize and celebrate their contributions.

How can I foster resilience in myself and others? I know we will encounter naysayers and real problems as we launch and implement our vision and strategies. The only thing I can think of is to use ABT to milk the setback for all it's worth. We need to learn lessons quickly and move on. No looking back.

How can I cultivate enough optimism and confidence to move ahead? We need to be relentless about charting our accomplishments along the way, no matter how small. We also need to give each other feedback on what we are saying and doing that moves things forward. We need to know how we can improve our leadership, but we don't need nitpicking criticism. I want to cultivate "yes we can!"

Step 5: The Supreme Ordeal

Diane can recall moments from the past when she and her team were able to prevail against all odds. Her memories in this step encourage others to recall similar situations and bolster her listeners' emotions and efforts to be successful. As they say, nothing succeeds like success!

> *How will we prevail against significant resistance and barriers?* We will help each other operate out of our signature strengths by reminding ourselves and each other which strengths have served us well in overcoming similar sources of resistance and barriers that we have encountered in the past. We will intentionally call on inner strengths such as determination, perseverance, empathy, creativity, and resilience, and encourage each other to show the conviction necessary to keep going.
>
> *How have we demonstrated resolve in similarly challenging situations?* I remember when we surprised ourselves by making the deadline to submit a proposal for special funding for dementia patients. Not only were we worried about the deadline, we were not sure we had made our case. We were successful on both fronts. What a high that was! We celebrated for weeks.

How will we find the strength and determination to stay the course? There is no doubt that our patience and determination will be tested. Achieving the vision will be a significant transition in attitude, behavior, and culture. I believe we need to showcase what is working and invite healthy competition so that other areas will strive to excel. We need to do the same thing for individuals. I will highlight significant individual effort and call others to a similar level of contribution.

Step 6: The Return Home

Notice in this step that Diane writes about the successes on the leadership and organizational levels as if they already happened. This is the mind-set that is crucial to stewarding success before it is actually realized. The leader needs to live the vision in his or her imagination well before it happens in real time.

How will we advance as never before? There is no question in my mind that I will hone my leadership skills to a level far beyond that which I have ever demonstrated. I believe I have been an excellent subject matter leader. After we complete this effort, I will know how to lead strategically. That goes for those in management positions too. There is a big difference between leading people to improve incrementally and leading people to create something brand new.

How will posterity remember us? We are striving to be a regional leader in continuum of care to the elderly.

We will know we are truly successful as others emulate what we have done.

How will we have fulfilled our destiny? We at St. Andrew's have a calling to set the standard in services to the elderly. By making these visionary changes, we will be fulfilling our destiny of:

- Being a trusted guide that advocates for elder residents under our care as their needs change over time

- Rewarding staff for their understanding of what every service across the spectrum provides and for recommending the appropriate set of services for the elder resident, even if the service is not in the mix

- Putting the needs of family members on par with that of elder residents under our care so that the experience of being at St. Andrew's is rewarding for all concerned

Crafting your Hero's Journey is one of the major stepping-stones to saying it with sizzle. You will be able to tell the whole story with a focus on the parts that are most relevant as your journey takes shape. The most important thing to remember is to see yourself, the leader, as the Hero and imagine the significant contributions that others will make along the way. This is a mental dress rehearsal for the real adventure to come. It will prepare you and your team to step into the challenges with the fullest attention, intention, and effort.

Saying it with sizzle paves the way to saying it with soul—the "why" of your vision and commitment. The soul of your message is the foundation of your listeners' trust in you as their leader. Explaining why it is so important to you gives personal meaning and purpose to your vision. In the next chapter, I guide you in moving from the how to the why for ultimate communication impact.

8

Say It with Soul

On July 4, 1939, Lou Gehrig, baseball's legendary first baseman, walked on the field at Yankee Stadium to give his farewell speech to the more than sixty-two thousand fans in attendance. Gehrig fought back tears as he thanked his fans, calling himself "the luckiest man on the face of this earth."[1]

Gehrig, thirty-five years old, was retiring from baseball because of a degenerative disease that would take his life two years later. His farewell speech that day went down in history. As you read his words, it is impossible not to feel his soul shining through. Now think of the impact they must have had on the crowd in the stadium as they listened to Gehrig speaking to them directly:

> Fans, for the past two weeks you have been reading about the bad break I got. Yet today I consider myself the luckiest man on the face of this earth. I have been

in ballparks for seventeen years and have never received anything but kindness and encouragement from you fans. Look at these grand men. Which of you wouldn't consider it the highlight of his career just to associate with them for even one day?

Sure, I'm lucky. Who wouldn't consider it an honor to have known Jacob Ruppert? Also, the builder of baseball's greatest empire, Ed Barrow? To have spent six years with that wonderful little fellow, Miller Huggins? Then to have spent the next nine years with that outstanding leader, that smart student of psychology, the best manager in baseball today, Joe McCarthy?

Sure, I'm lucky. When the New York Giants, a team you would give your right arm to beat, and vice versa, sends you a gift—that's something. When everybody down to the groundskeepers and those boys in white coats remember you with trophies—that's something. When you have a wonderful mother-in-law who takes sides with you in squabbles with her own daughter—that's something.

When you have a father and a mother who work all their lives so you can have an education and build your body—it's a blessing. When you have a wife who has been a tower of strength and shown more courage than you dreamed existed—that's the finest I know. So I close in saying that I may have had a tough break, but I have an awful lot to live for. Thank you.[2]

Why do you think Gehrig's words continue to inspire almost eighty years after the fact? First, Gehrig tackled the greatest of all paradoxical truths head-on: life is fragile, but at the same time it is rich and rewarding. He chose to emphasize the rich and rewarding assets of being alive over the daunting aspects of facing death. His asset-based thinking (ABT) perspective was that his blessings far outweighed his bad breaks. This is a seminal evaluation that we all must make. And subconsciously or not, we crave role models like Gehrig who show us that life in the end is most certainly well worth the ride. We want to identify with Gehrig as he iterates what makes him feel lucky and grateful versus what makes him feel down and out.

Second, Lou Gehrig's display of soul over the life span of his career played a significant role in the impact of his parting message. Gehrig was a star record-breaking player but he was just as well known for his reliability. Sports writer John Kieren of the *New York Times* wrote, "His greatest record doesn't show in the book. It was the absolute reliability of Henry Louis Gehrig. He could be counted upon. He was there every day at the ballpark bending his back and ready to break his neck to win for his side."[3] Gehrig walked on to the field that day as a man of character and a reminder that people are influenced by who you are as a human being, above and beyond what you have achieved.

As we learn more about how to say it with soul, let us keep these leadership lessons from Gehrig's "luckiest man" speech top of mind:

- The ABT perspective is inspirational, especially in the face of daunting circumstances.

- You earn the respect and trust of your constituents by baring your soul over time—that is, by the character and conduct you display on a daily basis.

Show Your Skin in the Game

It is worth repeating here that saying it with soul is about meaning what you say—and saying something meaningful. This can be a tall order for leaders, even when the core of the message is something positive. Why is it so difficult? First, it exposes your vulnerability. Whenever you communicate what something means to you, you are revealing something important about yourself. The second answer is related to a sense of false modesty. Leaders, like everyone else, are taught to be humble and not to draw undue positive attention to themselves. We are socialized not to brag and to view ego as a turn-off. But authentic humility is about having the confidence and transparency to own and express the best of who we are, as well as being able to admit our failures and shortcomings.

Often leaders think their teams are not concerned with what the leaders think is important; people only care about why something is important to their own well-being. That statement is true. People do care most about their own well-being, but that is why they need to know that the leaders they are about to follow have personal skin in the game. If a trusted leader is genuinely committed and personally invested in a cause, then it lowers the bar for his or her followers to get on board.

People have a built-in Geiger counter as to whether leaders are being true to what they value, and showing your skin in the game creates authenticity over time. For example, Lou Gehrig's dedication to the game of baseball over seventeen years is what made his retirement message all the more meaningful and soulful. Leading with soul is not just a matter of what you do and say in the moment; it is what you do and say over many moments—the high points, the low points, and all the other points in between. When it comes to saying it with soul, you, not your words, are the message.

Leaders Who Say It with Soul

What do the following high-profile leaders share in common?

Aung San Suu Kyi

Nelson Mandela

Desmond Tutu

Dr. Martin Luther King Jr.

Mother Teresa

I believe the primary attribute they share is a devotion to a mighty cause, a sense of purpose, a noble calling that is in true service of the welfare of others. When a leader is genuinely committed to and can effectively communicate his or her mighty cause, it is truly inspiring.

Aung San Suu Kyi is chairperson of Myanmar's National League for Democracy. Her famous soul-bearing message begins, "It is not power that corrupts, but fear. Fear of losing power corrupts those who wield it, and fear of the scourge of power corrupts those who are subject to it."[4] Over her lifetime in the political spotlight, she has shown her undying commitment to the mighty cause of freedom from fear. As an opposition politician, she was detained under house arrest for almost two decades, becoming one of the world's most prominent political prisoners. In 1991, she was awarded the Nobel Peace Prize for her "non-violent struggle for democracy and human rights." In 2012, she was awarded the US Congressional Gold Medal, the highest civilian honor bestowed by the United States.

During the Congressional Gold Medal awards ceremony, Senator John McCain delivered an emotional tribute thanking "the lady for teaching me at my age a thing or two about courage." Shortly after the ceremony, *New York Times* columnist Tom Friedman wrote of Suu Kyi: "So few leaders now dare to throw caution and polls to the wind and tell people the truth about anything hard or controversial. Aung San Suu Kyi gave up twenty years of her life for her country. Many leaders today won't even give up a news cycle."[5]

These comments highlight the positive and energizing effect of espousing a mighty cause. John McCain and Tom Friedman, both leaders in their own spheres, testify to being guided and inspired by Suu Kyi's soulful words and actions.

You may be wondering what having a mighty cause has to do with leading a business, a school, or a hospital. The answer is, "Everything." When you are able to link your vision and goals to a greater purpose, people are inspired. You help them grasp the true meaning of what you are trying to accomplish.

How Leading with Soul Can Inspire a New Sense of Pride: The Peabody Story

In 2013, I attended the World Forum of Jesuit Business Schools hosted by the St. Louis University School of Business in my home town. The luncheon keynote speaker was Andy Savitz, author of the best-seller, *The Triple Bottom Line: How Today's Best-Run Companies Are Achieving Economic, Social, and Environmental Success . . . and How You Can Too.*[6] Savitz told the audience how he felt about sustainability—that it was more than just economic stability for future generations. He defined it as the confluence of three powerful forces: economic sustainability (profit), environmental sustainability (caring for the planet), and social sustainability (caring for the people of the world). What he was talking about was the ultimate mighty cause: true sustainability. Now that's a greater purpose we can all rally around.

Savitz's remarks reminded me of the Peabody Energy Global Leadership Summit I facilitated in 2011, where I witnessed Greg Boyce, chairman and chief executive office of Peabody Energy, inspire over two hundred company leaders from around the world with his mighty cause for Peabody of true sustainability in terms of access to energy.

Peabody Energy is the world's largest private sector coal company and a global leader in advanced coal technologies and solutions. The title of Greg's speech that day was "Equal Energy Access: The Power of Coal." I watched the audience's positive reaction as he outlined the enormous societal problem that he called global energy poverty—according to him, over half of the global population lacks adequate access to energy—and the contributions that Peabody Energy was making to eliminate it.

Later I asked Greg what led him to the mighty cause of alleviating global energy poverty. He said:

> Today, Peabody is a highly effective organization. We are good at the basics of block and tackling when it comes to mining coal. We lead the world in safety and we are set to weather the economic cycles in our business. But there are negatives in our industry right now. Environmental activists are critical of carbon-dioxide emissions. Unions are vocal about their agendas. In general, coal has often had a somewhat backward-looking, rather than forward-looking, reputation.
>
> I want to combat those negatives and change our reputation by giving our employees a vision and a view of what we are doing to fundamentally improve the world. Our employees deserve to work in a company that is profitable and committed to improving society and supporting the environment—and they do.
>
> I want our employees to know that as a company, we are working hard to deploy next-generation clean coal technologies that achieve near-zero emissions. They are performing the work that helps billions of people live longer and better. Communicating this profound message to all of our stakeholders is one of my most important responsibilities. I want Peabody employees to have the strength of their convictions that we can and will reach our goal of electricity access for all by 2050.

As Greg and I continued our discussion, I remembered the high levels of engagement and participation from the leaders who attended the Peabody Global Summit. Greg's speech turned out to be the highlight of the conference for most attendees. I asked him two years later if he believed his leaders were still inspired by his soulful message. He replied:

> Now, more than ever. Our leaders and many of our employees are better able to have in-depth conversations with their family, friends, and neighbors about what Peabody is contributing to the world. I believe those dialogues are happening because they are proud to work at a company that truly has a noble mission.
>
> What is more, staying committed to the goal of true energy sustainability has made us more resilient and has helped us work harder to be successful, even in this economically harsh environment.

Small Shifts in Soulfulness, Big Difference in Satisfaction

It is not as difficult as you may think to discover the mighty cause underlying your vision for your organization. Recently I worked with a business leader who had decided to leave her job at an engineering company. For years, Stephanie had been successful in heading up operations: her costs were low and her productivity high. As we worked together to figure out her next steps, we developed her leadership life map, an ABT leadership tool that I introduce later in the chapter. Once

Stephanie studied the patterns revealed in the map, she realized that her deepest satisfaction came from mentoring others, not efficient operations. Getting results was of course rewarding, but her greatest reward came from watching people grow and excel. Training and developing people became her mighty cause as she established herself as a consultant who puts clients' growth center stage. And as with Suu Kyi, her unbridled dedication to what she feels born to do helps to inspire those she seeks to serve.

So don't fret if your mighty cause isn't world peace or eliminating global poverty. Soulful leadership happens on many levels.

Say It with Soul Self-Tests

These tests are designed to reveal strengths and areas for improvement in crafting a soulful message and delivering it in ways that motivate and inspire.

Rate yourself on the following two assessments using the 5-point scale: 5 = Excellent, 4 = Very Good, 3 = Average, 2 = Needs Improvement, 1 = Novice.

Here's how to calculate your assessment results. For any item you gave yourself a 4 or 5, mark those as your strong suits. For any item you gave yourself a 3, 2, or 1, mark those as areas for improvement. Select and concentrate on one area for improvement from each assessment: content and delivery. Remember, the content assessment items primarily target how you craft the content of your message, and the delivery assessment items focus on how you show up when you present your message.

Table 8.1 Lead Positive Soul Content Assessment

When I speak, I . . .	Excellent	Very Good	Average	Needs Improvement	Novice
Speak about my values and beliefs relative to the vision I am trying to accomplish.	5	4	3	2	1
Am transparent about my motives and intentions.	5	4	3	2	1
Connect my vision to a mighty cause and to listeners' values and sense of purpose.	5	4	3	2	1
Give examples of my willingness to make personal sacrifices and to put the vision and my listeners' well-being ahead of my own self-interest.	5	4	3	2	1
Acknowledge the contributions of others and show them how they will grow as they pursue the vision.	5	4	3	2	1

Table 8.2 Lead Positive Soul Delivery Assessment

When I speak, I . . .	Excellent	Very Good	Average	Needs Improvement	Novice
Emphatically express why the vision is important and meaningful to me.	5	4	3	2	1
Read the listeners' reactions in real time and value their comments.	5	4	3	2	1
Humbly ask people for their commitment, support, and willingness to sacrifice for the sake of achieving the vision.	5	4	3	2	1
Project an image of unshakable courage and resolve by standing still and being calm.	5	4	3	2	1
Demonstrate my authority by assuming an open, receptive posture—even when someone pushes back.	5	4	3	2	1

How to Say It with Soul

Soul is something you already have—it is your values and beliefs, your character, your mighty cause, your unique, authentic leadership presence in the world. Communicating with soul is a matter of revealing and demonstrating what you already have. This makes saying it with soul a much different proposition from saying it with substance or sizzle.

As you already know, substance (the what) must be logical and rational. You must provide a well-developed argument for the case for change. You must carefully think through the benefits for all stakeholders. There are external standards by which the substance of your message can be judged. The same holds true for sizzle (the how). When you tell the story, strategy, and road map, people immediately can assess how plausible your plan is, as well as how passionate you are about leading the effort.

When it comes to soul (the why), we are talking about something highly subjective—the meaning, the value, and the deeper purpose that underlie your commitment to the cause. People listening are scanning for how sincere, congruent, and authentic you are. Your team is taking a good look at you to judge how much they can trust you.

Recent research in neuroscience, spearheaded by Paul Zak, founding director of the Center for Neuroeconomic Studies at Claremont Graduate University, points to evidence that the hormone oxytocin, which is responsible for social recognition and bonding, is secreted at greater levels when a leader cares about the well-being of his or her constituents. That is, if the people you lead trust that you are looking out for them, their loyalty to you and to your cause is strengthened.[7]

It is important to remember that people will also tune into your body language and facial expressions to evaluate your authenticity. Communications research indicates that your visual presence, your body language, is a major influence on how trustworthy you appear.[8] These two findings underline the power of the soul asset when it comes to building bonds of trust.

My Sincerity Profile

The more aware you are of when you are perceived by others as sincere and authentic, the more intentional you can be about demonstrating those qualities. The following ABT feedback exercise helps increase your awareness of these occasions by seeking feedback from trusted members of your circle.

Identify five people who have regular contact with you. Ask each person to answer the following questions:

- Can you recall an instance when you felt I was speaking sincerely and authentically? What was the subject? How could you tell I was sincere?
- Can you recall a time when I was demonstrating my commitment to a cause I believe in? What was I saying and doing? How could you sense my commitment?
- Under what circumstances would you like me to display more sincerity or authenticity?

Look for themes within the responses that offer insight into when and how you say it with soul. Intentionally integrate messages that highlight your sincerity and authenticity into your conversations and presentations.

The patterns from this sincerity feedback process may surprise you. For instance, one sales executive who prided himself on his self-confidence found out, to his surprise, that it was when he opened up about his struggles that people saw him as most sincere and authentic. His respondents recommended that he reveal his critical thinking process when trying to sell to a potential customer. For this sales leader, all he needed was the feedback about letting people into his thought process. There was no new skill he needed to develop; it was simply a matter of being more open and transparent. That is precisely what saying it with soul is all about.

Use this exercise to discover when you come across as most sincere and most authentic. Armed with a new level of insight, you can do what the sales executive did: reveal the true essence of you.

My Leadership Life Map

Another way to tap into your most soulful self is to examine the leadership moments that have shaped who you are and what matters most to you. The leader you are today is a direct result of multiple variables. The fabric of your life has been woven from individual life experiences, relationships, challenges, and choices. Reflecting on the whole of your life at a macrolevel can help you see important patterns and themes. It can also help you identify sources of inspiration and blind spots. Following is a condensed version of the leadership life map exercise for the purposes of this chapter. To download the full exercise, go to drkathycramer.com.

Step 1

Identify and describe five major life-shaping forces that have left a lasting impression on you and influenced how you lead others. Examples of life-shaping forces are mentors; family dynamics; personal, academic, and professional milestones and losses.

Step 2

Map the chapters of your life as a leader. For example:

Chapter 1: School age

Chapter 2: College plus early career

Chapter 3: Early career to midcareer

Chapter 4: Midcareer to present

Within each chapter, list your most significant leadership experiences. Include the life-shaping forces you already identified in step 1. You can also use this list to help organize your thoughts:

- Proudest achievements
- Regrettable decisions
- Episodes of misfortune
- Unexpected opportunities
- Seized opportunities

- Learning moments
- Setbacks

As an example, table 8.3 contains some of the highlights from the leadership life map of Stephanie, whom we met earlier in the chapter, a business leader who left her operations position at an engineering company to pursue her passion of helping and mentoring people as a consultant. To create your own leadership life map, go to drkathycramer.com for a free blank template.

Observe the theme of serving and developing people over Stephanie's leadership life map. Also clearly apparent are the many business operation achievements across her career. When Stephanie examined the highlights and hurdles of her leadership career, she realized she was recognized and promoted primarily for her business acumen and operational competencies. However, at this next stage in her career, she wanted to emphasize her people development leadership skills. That insight led Stephanie to explore the feasibility of starting her own consulting firm. And that is exactly what she did.

Step 3

For each significant leadership experience, describe the key assets you used or noticed in others in order to capitalize on that event. Note their impact on yourself, others, and the situation. Look for themes and patterns in your leadership competencies.

Step 4

Select a few signature leadership moments that have formed your values and beliefs. Use them to craft a story that reveals

Table 8.3 Stephanie's Leadership Life Map

	School Age	College Plus Two Years	Early Career	Midcareer to Present
Proudest achievements	Senior year changed from softball to tennis. Was #2 player and captain of the team	Graduated top student in business school Led mentor program to ensure high school seniors were prepared for entering college	Lived 2 years working in Japan on joint venture for construction company	Led a $300 million global business, generated 65% market share in health care construction
Regrettable decisions	Could have been top of the class if I had studied			Turned down assignment in China; have some regrets

Opportunities and learning moments	Faith walk: Mission trips to help homeless in Denver and Detroit	Spoke to 250 high school seniors about charting their own course, got standing ovation. Met my husband	Achieved significant cost reductions in construction operations. Hired and developed 4 new ops managers	Elected to school board. Was able to shift from $500,000 negative cash flow to $1 million positive cash flow
Setbacks		Became distant from my parents		
Life-shaping forces	Grandmother was incredible woman who believed in me and instilled value for helping others	Dean of business school encouraged me to apply for key internships in construction industry	My boss, the COO, gave me opportunity to on-board new hires and lead a culture change process	

who you are, what you believe in, and why your mighty cause is so meaningful to you. Make sure the story exposes your past vulnerability as well as your leadership strengths. Use the Hero's Journey template from chapter 7 to ensure you imbue the story with soul *and* sizzle.

Self-Others-Situation Framework for Saying It with Soul

Once you have begun to craft your soulful message, I recommend you run it through our tried-and-true Self-Others-Situation framework to ensure your words speak directly to the situation and the people (yourself and others) that matter the most.

Self

Identify what you want to be meaningful and inspiring in your message. Review the list of speech acts that relate specifically to the asset of soul and decide which ones are most relevant to your message.

Soul-Oriented Speech Acts

    Promise

    Commit

    Trust

    Resolve

    Pledge

    Hope

Guarantee

Fulfill

Inspire

Believe

Soul-oriented speech acts will help you connect on the human-to-human "why" level. Notice how each of the words on this list reflects your values and character, as well as the underlying importance of your message. I recommend you use the pronoun "I" often—I pledge, I believe, I am committed, I am inspired—as you craft your messages. The soulful speech acts you claim with "I" help you signal to listeners your deepest purpose. Note the power of Tom Friedman's words on Suu Kyi: "I love this line: It's not power, but the fear of losing power that corrupts."[9]

Others

How does the message you are about to deliver relate to your mighty cause? Why is this message meaningful to the group? Why should your audience commit themselves to supporting this effort? Which values and beliefs does it serve? How does your message inspire a deep sense of purpose in others?

With substance, you give others a clear call to action. With sizzle, you offer others an invitation to feel. And now with soul, you provide others meaning and purpose. This story highlights the role of soul in communicating and connecting with others:

A stranger walks up to a group of laborers and asks, "What are you doing?"

Laborer 1 says, "Laying bricks."

Laborer 2 says, "Building a wall."

Laborer 3 says, "Constructing a cathedral."

Laborer 4 says, "Doing God's work."

Moral of the story: If you want to inspire the fourth level of meaning, you must offer that deeper sense of purpose to others.

Situation

Timeliness can contribute substantially to the meaning and value of your message. You can easily see how the timing of Lou Gehrig's soulful farewell speech added to its meaning. The fans had heard about Gehrig's diagnosis about two weeks before the speech. He was convinced it was time to retire before his illness sabotaged his game. His fans and teammates respected Gehrig's swift public acknowledgment of his "bad break" news and decision to leave the game.

You have heard the phrase, "timing is everything." This adage is especially true when it comes to communicating soulfully. Look through the situation lens to determine how best to capture why your message is so important at this moment in time.

The situation at hand also provides you with ideas about how to position the message. Consider the following situational factors related to timing.

- Overdue circumstances
- An urgent matter
- A perfect moment

- A chance to get ahead of the curve
- Being ahead (or behind) at halftime
- An overtime situation

How the leader sees the time factor can spur people to action. Using the asset of timing is one more situational variable you can use to increase your communication effectiveness.

Soul in Action

In chapter 5, I introduced in table 5.1 the Lead Positive communication road map to explain substance, sizzle, and soul in terms of what you say and how you say it. Take another look at the table, focusing in particular on the soul section.

Following up on the St. Andrew's Resources for Seniors System leadership team, we will review how they used the soul section of the chart to strengthen their vision message of a new, more effective system for providing health care services to the elderly.

The leadership team, comprising CEO Mary Alice Ryan, COO Diane Meatheany, and CFO Greg Elliott brainstormed their responses to each "why" on the chart. Here is what they came up with:

- Why this is so important to the bigger picture:

  Senior services needs an overhaul.

  We can be a role model and industry leader.

  Seniors are the fastest-growing generation. Plus, their increasing life expectancy means their need for our services will grow.

Table 8.4 The Lead Positive Communication Road Map

	What You Say	How You Say It
Substance	What must be accomplished: • The case for change • The positive vision of the future What I want to make you, the listener, understand What the benefits will be for: • Followers • The organization • The community, industry, the world	Authoritatively Confidently Convincingly Clearly Rationally
Sizzle	How we will get there: • The strategy • The road map • The story How we will work together to: • Forge alliances • Neutralize opposition • Recognize contributions • Overcome obstacles • Solicit help and guidance • Navigate ups and downs	Passionately Empathetically Invitingly Energetically Openly
Soul	Why this is important to: • The bigger picture • Our values and beliefs • Our organization Why this is so important: • To me (my skin in the game) • To my commitment • For you to be involved	Sincerely Vulnerably Inspirationally Congruently Inspiringly

- Why this is so important to our values and beliefs:

  We believe seniors deserve access to excellent service regardless of their income level.

  We are dedicated to providing the most efficient, effective, and innovative range of services.

  We treat seniors in our managed facilities as valued customers.

- Why this is so important to our organization:

  The new matrixed team approach will ensure seamless service.

  This vision will ensure the financial sustainability of St. Andrew's.

  This vision will empower employees and help managers develop new leadership skills in strategy development and change management.

- Why this is so important to me (my skin in the game):

  I love working at St. Andrew's, and I want to make sure it continues to be around.

  I want to learn to lead the strategy and get out of the day-to-day tactics.

  This is a chance for me to take my business acumen to the next level.

- Why this is so important to my commitments:

  I am committed to continuous improvement.

  I am committed to the sustainability of this organization.

  I am committed to achieving breakthrough results.

I am committed to this leadership team's success and effectiveness.

- Why it is important for you to be involved:

We need leadership at all levels to champion the new vision.

We need your ideas and input on how to create and execute the new strategy.

We need you to inspire and motivate others.

As a leader, you might want to take a page out of the St. Andrew's leadership playbook when it comes to defining the "whys" behind the "what." Mary Alice, Diane, and Greg completed this exercise together because they wanted to hear and adopt each other's "whys." You may also benefit from working with members of your team and other key stakeholders to weigh in on their "whys."

Revealing your "why"—that is, saying it with soul—gives others a reason to trust you, trust the process, and believe in the meaning and importance of your message. Saying it with soul gives you a sound platform from which to lead and paves the way for taking action that is also meaningful and authentic. Your soulful connection to your message, your values and mighty cause, and your followers will set the stage for the authentic leadership actions that will help drive success. Next, we explore the ABT strategies for those authentic leadership actions in part 3, "What Highly Effective Leaders Do."

PART 3

What Highly Effective Leaders Do

Start a positive ripple effect

9

From Say to Do

It's a Very Short Trip

The brain, it seems, does not make much of a distinction between second- and firsthand experiences. Whether you're doing something or watching someone else do the same thing, the same neurological regions in your brain are stimulated. This phenomenon has been illuminated by recent findings in neuroscience and cognitive and social psychology. Research shows that the same pattern of neurons, called mirror neurons, fires in the observer as in the person performing a task or telling a story.[1]

Neuroscientists attribute the understanding of the goals, desires, intentions, feelings, and actions of others in large measure to the mirror neuron system. Cognitive and social psychologists have found that mirror neurons also give humans the ability to see others' points of views—what they call *theory of mind*.[2] A theory of mind about others allows us to empathize with their experiences. It is developed through social interactions and secondhand observations that depict the complexities of social life. Introspection is how we develop a theory of mind about ourselves. Mirroring the actions and language of others also develops our ability for introspection, which leads to increased self-awareness and a deeper ability to understand our own experiences.

According to neurologist V. S. Ramachandran, the director of the Center for Brain and Cognition at the University of California, San Diego, the imitation function of mirror neurons and their role in our development of theories of mind is responsible for the evolution of complex skill in humans, such as tool making, using fire, building shelters, and language development. Because of mirror neurons, these complex skills spread horizontally through the population and vertically into future generations, thus shaping culture and civilization.[3]

Now, let's apply this knowledge to the leadership sphere. When you perform an act of leadership, the same neurons that fire in your brain will fire in the brains of your team members. Thanks to mirror neurons, the *do*—and the feeling or tone behind that *do*—is highly contagious. The mirror neurons of your listeners mirror your leadership actions, initiating the process of imitative learning and spreading cultural norms and behaviors throughout the team.

These findings highlight the asset-based thinking (ABT) principle that leaders must set the example for what they want their followers to see, say, and do. When the leader is enthusiastic, team members will respond with a similarly high level of positive energy. If the leader's brain is in the responsive, creative mode, followers' brains are more likely to operate that way too. The negative corollary is also true: what the leader does in the reactive, high-alert stress mode will trigger a similar high-alert reaction in followers.

The See-Say-Do Chain Reaction

The See-Say-Do chain reaction starts with you as the leader. What you see influences your desires, intentions, goals, and actions. Asset-based or deficit-based thinking: it's entirely up to you. What you say—through substance, sizzle, and soul—lets others place themselves in your mental shoes. The ability to see from your point of view allows them to develop a theory of mind about who you are as a leader and what you hope to achieve. What you do leads others to imitate your actions and develop the complex skills that form the culture of your team. Take a look at the following example.

Ten years ago, Tom Voss, then the chief operating officer of Ameren, the parent company of the utilities Ameren Missouri and Ameren Illinois, saw issues with the company's safety record and its lack of a safety mind-set and culture. At the conclusion of an all-hands-on-deck leadership meeting, Tom decided to ignite a sense of urgency and inspire a commitment to safety in the over two hundred leaders in attendance by saying and doing something unexpected and well out of his comfort zone. His story is a perfect illustration of the See-Say-Do chain reaction and the courage it takes to lead effectively:

See. Tom visualized a future in which Ameren had a perfect safety record: zero injuries and zero fatalities. He saw that it was possible if leaders at all levels of the company adopted a safety mind-set and created a culture that rewarded and prioritized safety.

Say. Tom related his vision directly to all the company leaders: "Ameren can achieve a perfect safety record if we all believe it is possible and we all put our minds to it. If we are committed to safety, our people will be committed to safety," he said. He also made the following pledge to safety:

1. "I will not commit an unsafe act.
2. "I will insist that my fellow employees not commit an unsafe act."
3. "I *commit* to safety!"

Do. Tom stood tall as he pledged his commitment to safety. Then he asked each of the leaders to stand with him, recite the pledge, and make the same commitment.

This public call to action was completely out of Tom's comfort zone. No one expected the naturally reserved Tom to stand up in front of this audience of leaders, make a bold commitment, and request that they stand with him and do the same. Tom's actions and leadership presence astounded his audience, and to this day, they remember that moment as the first monumental step on the road to becoming a company that sees safety as its number one job. I believe that the symbolic action Tom took by standing up, and then asking others to stand with him, underscored the weight of the commitment they were making and helped them to maintain the fierce resolve needed to making Tom's vision a reality.

Today Tom is Ameren's CEO. The company is in the top 10 percent of the industry in terms of safety records, and its safety culture is exemplary. In this story, what the leaders saw (Tom's vision for a perfect safety record), what they said (their public pledge to put safety first), and what they did (stand together to symbolize their commitment to each other and to achieving this unified vision) led to amazingly effective results.

A Virtuous Cycle

It is also important to note that what your followers see, say, and do can and should influence your leadership actions. Your job as leader includes being aware of and receptive to what others are seeing, saying, and doing. By focusing first on creating your own asset-based See-Say-Do cycle, however, you can initiate a positive chain reaction that makes it easier to monitor and manage the See-Say-Do interactions throughout your team.

As you will learn in the chapters to follow, what you *do* as a consequence of your ABT focus (*see*) and your ABT communication (*say*) will incorporate being receptive and responsive to others. You will learn how to constantly monitor the conscious intentions behind your actions to ensure what you *do* remains aligned with what you *see* and *say*. In this way, you will give a whole new meaning to the phrase "walking the talk."

In chapter 10, we focus on the actions of responsive leaders—those who take the time to think and do intentionally in the face of stressful and disturbing events. In chapter 11, we explore the relationship between being and doing when it comes to highly effective leadership. The focus of chapter 12 will be on what to do to drive transformational change. And in chapter 13, we come full circle to see exactly how the See-Say-Do connection works to give you the asset-based leadership advantage.

10

Reactive or Responsive

It's Up to You

In psychological terms, *responding* means to thoughtfully and intentionally adapt your behavior to the current circumstance. It involves the parasympathetic nervous system, which is activated when the body is calm and at rest. In contrast, *reacting* means to automatically go into high-alert stress mode. Your brain automatically processes the problem as a state of emergency and your sympathetic nervous system is activated, preparing your body to fight, flee, or freeze.

Highly effective leaders tend to be highly responsive leaders. They take the time to digest what is happening, step back and take stock, and exude high energy and excitement, not fear and stress. Thanks to the mirror neuron phenomenon, people follow their lead and are responsive in return.

A leader's actions telegraph what is happening internally— high energy or high alert. Of course, it is not possible to always be completely calm under stressful conditions. In a difficult situation, a deficit-based reactive mind-set is natural at first. But if you can shift into responsive mode, you can choose to channel your adrenaline to serve you. Respond or react: it's up to you.

The Wider the Lens, the Better the View

Last year I worked with two leaders who embodied the reactive and responsive modes. Mr. Reactive had been referred to me for coaching by his boss, Mr. Responsive. Everyone working within earshot of Mr. Reactive was so stressed out because of his belligerent behavior that they were threatening to quit. Mr. Responsive made it very clear: Mr. Reactive had to lose the aggression or lose his job.

Mr. Reactive was somewhat apologetic, but not really. He felt that those around him should know that he was just standing up for what he thought was right. He told me, "At the first sign of a disagreement, I go into high gear and say and do whatever it takes to win the argument. I have had to deal with people who always bullied their way out of a disagreement. Now I'm a hard-ass too."

Early in the coaching process, I met with both men. I asked Mr. Responsive to tell me exactly how he wanted to see Mr. Reactive behave in the face of disagreements or conflicts. Mr. Responsive wanted to see respectful, considerate behavior in the process of coming to a resolution. To help Mr. Reactive gain some insight into what drives respectful and considerate behavior, I asked his boss to tell me what he himself was thinking when he had a conflict or disagreement with someone. Mr. Responsive told me he first thought about how important the business was and then how valuable the person he disagreed with was to the success of the business. I stopped him from going any further and asked Mr. Reactive what he thought about his boss's frame of mind in response to conflict.

Mr. Reactive was caught completely off guard. He finally said, "All I think about is how to win the argument. I certainly don't think about the business or how valuable the person is to the success of the business." We then discussed how critical it is to widen the lens of what you are focusing on—that is, what you see—during a conflict. As we discussed in the previous chapter, once you can shift what you see toward the positive and possible, the say and do will automatically follow. Mr. Reactive saw only the disagreement, while Mr. Responsive saw the much bigger picture of the success of the business and the value of the other person. A wider lens does not resolve conflict, but it does broaden one's perspective so that it becomes much easier to channel the adrenaline of the moment toward a high-energy response rather than a high-alert reaction.

Gradually Mr. Reactive learned to broaden his perspective by imitating his boss and simulating his asset-based thinking (ABT) strategies for being responsive. He brought to mind what he valued most about the person he was in disagreement with and that person's value to the business. These positive and constructive thoughts slowed his reaction time so he could take stock before choosing a response.

Of course, Mr. Reactive's new strategy did not work perfectly every time. But because he went public with his commitment to be more respectful and collaborative, people gave him the time and space to learn his new approach. After about four weeks of practicing widening the lens, Mr. Reactive confided in me that being responsive increased his confidence and gave him a sense of being more in control of himself and his interactions. And that is precisely the goal of this chapter: learning how to respond effectively so that what you do as a leader takes you and the team further toward the goals you seek.

Reading Your Body in Real Time

Your body can be your most trusted ally in evaluating whether you are on track to respond or to react. As we have discussed, your body and facial expressions reveal your internal state. When you are primed internally to fight, you frown, grimace, pace, fidget, clench your teeth, and even sometimes pound the table. When you are primed internally to flee, you may have that deer-in-the-headlights look: your face is flushed; you turn away and even cringe or cower. In contrast, when you are primed to engage, you appear relaxed yet energetic. Your face and posture convey openness and a sense of positive expectancy. You lean in, not away from.

For decades, psychologists have known that by shifting your behavior, you can change your internal state, and vice versa.[1] Like most other people, you exhibit distinct and unique patterns of behavior when you are in responsive and reactive modes. A keen awareness of what happens when you are angry, afraid, energized, or engaged is key to making that shift from responding to reacting when necessary. This next test helps to increase your awareness of your specific behavioral patterns.

In tables 10.1 and 10.2, circle the number that reflects how frequently you experience these signs of responsiveness and

Table 10.1 Signs of Adrenaline Responsiveness

When I'm in a stressful situation, I feel . . .	Almost Always	Often	Sometimes	Rarely	Almost Never
1. Enthusiastic	5	4	3	2	1
2. Hopeful	5	4	3	2	1
3. Engaged	5	4	3	2	1
4. Energetic	5	4	3	2	1
5. Curious	5	4	3	2	1
6. Resilient	5	4	3	2	1
7. Creative	5	4	3	2	1
8. Proactive	5	4	3	2	1
9. Open-minded	5	4	3	2	1

Table 10.2 Signs of Adrenaline Reactivity

When I'm in a stressful situation, I feel . . .	Almost Always	Often	Sometimes	Rarely	Almost Never
1. Frustrated	5	4	3	2	1
2. Anxious	5	4	3	2	1
3. Closed-minded	5	4	3	2	1
4. Angry	5	4	3	2	1
5. Tense	5	4	3	2	1
6. Hyperactive	5	4	3	2	1
7. Worried	5	4	3	2	1
8. Indecisive	5	4	3	2	1
9. Self-critical	5	4	3	2	1

reactivity in the face of stressful situations. Then calculate what your scores show:

Add up your points for 1 through 9 for table 10.1. Total score _____

What Your Responsiveness Score Shows
36–45   Substantial responsiveness
21–35   Moderate responsiveness
9–20   Minimal responsiveness

Add up your points for 1 through 9 for table 10.2. Total score _____

What Your Reactivity Score Shows
36–45   Substantial reactivity
21–35   Moderate reactivity
9–20   Minimal reactivity

This questionnaire is designed to remind you that adrenaline serves two masters: responsiveness and reactivity. Reflect on the patterns of your internal signals so that you can quickly assess which track you are on the next time you encounter a stressful situation.

Download copies of these tests at drkathycramer.com, and ask one or two close friends or colleagues to fill them out. This will help you get a better understanding of how others view your responses.

Asset-Based Thinking Leadership Strategies for Responsiveness

Remember the lesson of mirror neurons: your behavior is contagious.[2] As a leader, when you are reactive and on high alert, your team is more likely to be reactive and stressed out. Conversely, when you respond intentionally to stress, team members are more likely to follow suit and engage the problem constructively. The asset-based stress management strategies that follow will help you increase your ability to be responsive while supporting you in lowering your reactivity.

Strategy 1: Take Ten

One of my favorite sayings is, "The only difference between fear and excitement is breathing." Adopt this phrase as a kind of mantra when you start to feel stress-induced anxiety coming on. The physical action (the do) of taking ten deep breaths will help you interrupt the high-alert cycle and channel your adrenaline positively toward high energy.

Try taking ten deep breaths when you would rather be excited than fearful. This creates a break in your reactivity, clearing the way for your parasympathetic nervous system to kick in. After all, you cannot be calm and anxious simultaneously.

Strategy 2: Get Off the Field and into the Stands

Think about the difference in perspective when you are a player on the field versus a spectator in the stands. As a player, you have a more immediate and narrower line of sight. In contrast, when you are in the stands, you can see what is happening on the whole field. Because your perspective is wider, you can track the movement of all the players and anticipate the plays.

In our day-to-day activity, we spend most of the time "on the field," intensely immersed in making the best plays to win the game. When the pressure gets too intense, you can reduce your anxiety and facilitate responsiveness by going "into the stands" to see the bigger picture. In psychology, we call this "going meta" to your circumstances. While you are still engaged in solving problems, making decisions, and other daily activities, you simultaneously rise above the situation to observe the dynamics. From that meta perspective, you can ask yourself questions like: What am I doing? How are others behaving? What is really going on here?

Going into the stands allows you to mentally extract yourself from your reactions and the immediate demands of the moment. From that more elevated perspective, you can better interpret the behavior of others to find the assets of the situation and see new possibilities. Going into the stands allows you to better develop theories of minds on the people around you and thereby understand what they are experiencing, adopt their points of view, and stand in their mental shoes.

Once you can empathize deeply with the intentions, desires, feelings, and behaviors of others, you understand better how to respond to the situation and adapt to their interests and needs—the mark of truly effective leadership.

Mark Eisenhart, an executive at Adayana, an agribusiness group, is one of the strongest asset-based leaders I know. He was the head of operations for Monsanto, the agricultural and biotechnology giant, when I first worked with him on developing his ABT mind-set.

Mark created a joint venture between Adayana and Zoetis (previously Pfizer Animal Health), called People First

Consulting Services, where he now serves as general manager. The new business works with farmers and ranchers on developing their businesses and their human capital. In these early stages, Mark has concentrated on creating demand for the venture's services because strategic planning, marketing, succession planning, and management development assistance are new to this target group.

Mark had to go into the stands to get the bigger picture of what his potential clients' needs were. He could immediately see that return on investment was the only measure that mattered to farm and ranch owners. But when it came to the interests and needs of the people managers, Mark and his team discovered a very different set of reinforcers. Most of the people in this group had been promoted from animal handling into talent management roles with virtually no experience with managing people. Nonetheless, they were as interested in maintaining a fun work environment with high job satisfaction as they were in return on investment and productivity.

To get business owners on board, Mark looked for first movers—early adopters willing to try out his services and provide testimonials on the positive impact on their bottom lines. To engage managers and supervisors, Mark worked on showing them the management skills People First Consulting Services could help them develop to improve work culture and retention.

One of the things I admire so much about Mark is his composure and enthusiasm. Executives in many start-ups, where the uncertainty of success is built in, quickly fall into reactive mode and stay there. Mark, however, was able to maintain his equanimity because he spent significant time off the field and in the stands. By putting himself in the mental shoes of owners and managers, Mark exercised his responsiveness in the face of start-up stressors. He developed theories of mind for both sets of customers so that he could engage them as assets in building his business.

Strategy 3: Act, Observe, Reflect

The extent to which you learn from your leadership experiences is key to increasing your effectiveness. This point was driven home to me shortly after graduate school when an executive I was working with gave me a copy of *Leadership: Enhancing the Lessons of Experience*, by Richard Hughes, Robert Ginnet, and Gordon Curphy.[3] In chapter 3 of this classic leadership text, I learned about the action-observation-reflection model. It resonated so strongly with me that I have used it in my work ever since.

The premise of the model is that once leaders commit an act, they must stop to observe what happened and then reflect on what was done well (or poorly) and what lessons they can carry forward. The model calls for leaders to learn from what they do. Taking the time to observe and reflect on your actions automatically puts you in the responsive mode. The benefits are also a well-earned time-out from doing and the cultivation of rich lessons for what to do better next time.

I asked Mark Eisenhart to tell me about his actions, observations, and reflections on his first year leading People First Consulting Services. He summarized for me each type of leadership action he had taken: writing the business plan, creating the training programs, identifying prospective customers, hiring consultants, getting the two joint customers to invest start-up funding, and so on. He made the observation that his results exceeded expectations in terms of revenue and number of customers. He also pointed to testimonials from customers on how their businesses improved because of People First's consulting services. Mark particularly reflected on just how important the skill of enrollment had been in driving a successful first year. Getting his team, bosses, potential clients, and other stakeholders on board was how he built the momentum to get the business off the ground. The power of enrollment was his biggest lesson, and he planned to continue emphasizing enrollment in years 2 and 3.

What Mark did in this example is what I want you to do more intentionally: assess what you are learning as a function of what you are doing. You can accomplish this in the privacy of your own thoughts, or process what you are learning out loud in conversation with someone else, as Mark did with me. Both methods work to help you milk your leadership experiences for all they are worth.

Memories Provide Momentum

Let's now explore how these three ABT stress management strategies work together.

1. Taking ten is key to shifting from a reactive to a responsive mode in the moment. It short-circuits your sympathetic nervous system activity just long enough so that you can begin to get off the field and into the stands.
2. When you go meta to the situation at hand, you can see the dynamics of what is happening more clearly. What you

do next is more effective because you are standing in the mental shoes of the people involved and you have the bigger picture of the assets in play.

3. Then, you use the act-observe-reflect process to build on your experience so that you can do even better next time.

Notice how each strategy is dedicated to helping you respond, not react, to stressful situations. Notice also how reflection plays an important role in both the second and third strategies. When you go into the stands, you are reflecting in real time about what to do that will be most effective in the moment. In the third strategy, you are reflecting retrospectively to inform your future actions. As our final work together in chapter 10, I want you to reward yourself by using the ABT tool from chapter 3, Scan-Snap-Savor, to imprint on your mind the benefits of using these ABT stress management strategies.

Scan for specific moments when you have given yourself time to catch your breath (strategy 1). Think of when you have mentally risen above what is happening to empathize with others and see more possibilities (strategy 2). Recall the times when you stepped back to review the leadership lessons to carry forward (strategy 3). *Snap* to create mind's-eye pictures of those moments complete with sensory details of the settings and your state of mind. *Savor* those experiences by dwelling for at least thirty seconds on the positive emotions they bring up.

I am asking you to scan, snap, and savor the times you have used these stress strategies so you realize that you already know how to do them. These are strategies, not complicated skills.

Now that you have names for each tool, examples from me, and examples from your own leadership efforts, you can more reliably and consistently put them to use. Remember the Aristotelian notion, "We are what we repeatedly do." When you repeatedly shift from reactive to responsive, what you do is repeatedly more effective. You already know what to do; all you have to do now is remember.

These stress management strategies aimed at fostering your ability to respond thoughtfully and effectively pave the way for chapter 11, which offers you more insights into the leader you already are. With a deeper sense of the leadership qualities you already possess, you can strengthen the link between who you are and what you do for highly effective and authentic leadership.

Start Being Before You Start Doing

It is difficult, in fact nearly impossible, to see yourself as you are. However, knowing the particular positive qualities that underscore your leadership effectiveness is what allows them to shine through in all that you do. As a leader, you must be rigorously introspective and at the same time open to feedback in order to develop a clear picture of who you are and how others experience you—what I like to call your signature presence. Just as we all have a unique way of signing our names, we all create a unique signature as leaders. Your signature presence is the unique suite of leadership assets that make you you.

When I Am at My Best: A Self-Reflection Tool

Holding up the mirror so you see your positive qualities helps you more fully understand your signature presence as a leader.

This three-step self-reflection tool helps you to become more aware of who you are when you are leading effectively:

Step 1: Complete the following stem sentence five times. Don't overthink your responses—just write down whatever first comes to mind:

When I am at my best, I am a leader who is
_____.

When I am at my best, I am a leader who is
_____.

When I am at my best, I am a leader who is
_____.

When I am at my best, I am a leader who is
_____.

When I am at my best, I am a leader who is
_____.

Step 2: Complete this sentence:

If I were an even more effective leader, I would be
_____.

Step 3: Ask one or two colleagues to reflect on your signature presence and complete steps 1 and 2 about your leadership style:

From step 1: When [your name] is at his/her best, he/she is a leader who is _____.

From step 2: If [your name] were an even more effective leader, he/she would be _____.

This sentence-completion process uses the five-to-one principle from chapter 1 to ensure your focus is on your leadership assets, not deficits. By generating five times more positive insights about your leadership than negative ones, you uncover the qualities of being that underlie your effectiveness as a leader. You obtain insight into how your beingness drives what you do. I recommend you use this tool about once a month to get in touch with your leadership qualities of being.

Recently I applied this ABT sentence-completion tool to myself. Here were my responses:

- When I am at my best, I am a leader who is:

  Relational

  Imaginative

  Enthusiastic

  Creative

  Articulate

- If I were an even more effective leader, I would be: Patient

When I examined my responses to the first five open-ended sentence stems, I could better see the qualities of being I have been tapping into the writing of this book.

- Being relational keeps me focused on what is most valuable to you, the reader, in understanding and practicing asset-based strategies and tools.

- Being imaginative relates to how I craft the leadership stories in this book. I actually imagine the events and interactions from the real-life stories while I am writing them.
- My enthusiastic quality of being keeps me going when it comes to the actual and sometimes tedious writing, researching, and editing of the manuscript for this book.
- Being creative keeps me open to fresh ideas about how to convey my message.
- Being articulate helps me choose the right words to best express what highly effective leaders see, say, and do.

As I reflect on the qualities of being relational, imaginative, enthusiastic, creative, and articulate, I can tap into them more intentionally. For example, I can focus on being even more relational by making a greater effort to stand in the mental shoes of my readers.

My insight into which quality of being would make me even more effective in writing this book (patience) applies to many of my leadership goals, not just writing. I have discovered that the more patient I am, the more thoughtful and responsive my behavior is. For me, being more patient leads to making better choices, and this then becomes a self-reinforcing process. I see "patient" come up again and again when I do this self-reflection. That tells me how important it is for me to concentrate on integrating this quality of being into my signature presence.

The Three Cs

Three qualities of being are vital to leading effectively in the three types of situations you are bound to face as a leader:

- Confident in response to a crisis
- Curious in response to conflict
- Courageous in response to challenges

Being Confident in Response to a Crisis

Leaders know that it is important to be confident in almost every leadership situation. However, the importance of this quality of being grows exponentially in times of crisis. A leader who is confident inspires hope and determination in others. The hope that equilibrium will be regained and that the organization will bounce back is essential when dealing with a crisis. Once again, remember the lessons of mirror neurons: the confidence you wear on your face and the confidence you express through your body language, words, and actions will be contagious. And that is exactly what you want.

Laura Herring founded and is now the chairwoman of IMPACT Group, a global firm that provides spousal and family relocation assistance and career transition and talent management professional services. I have gotten to know Laura well over the past six years as a colleague and a friend. In my eyes, Laura has always exuded confidence. Confidence is part of her signature presence and has contributed to her considerable success as a leader and entrepreneur.

What I did not know about Laura was the important role her confidence played in the launch of her business. I heard all about it when I attended a keynote speech she was giving to other successful women in business. She began by taking the audience back to 1987, when she first identified an unmet need that she could fill. As a psychologist, Laura had heard firsthand from many of her clients that their family lives were turned upside down when they had to uproot their spouses and children and move to new cities for work. The stress of relocation was lowering productivity and retention for the companies of these clients.

Armed with a mighty cause, as she said, to "save families," Laura developed the first program in the United States to support families in the process of relocation. As a result, a new industry was born: family relocation transition services. Companies worldwide have since adopted her relocation programs. In 1987, however, no company had ever contemplated buying relocation counseling and support for employees and their family members. Far from being met, this need had barely even been recognized.

As a new business, Laura double-mortgaged her home to fulfill her first customer order for employee relocation program support kits from the CEO of a global company that moved over a thousand employees a year among its locations. Laura thought that the handshake of the executive vice president of the company was sufficient to close the $1 million order. It wasn't. After closing her private practice and consulting business, spending eighteen months developing her family relocation transition program, and double-mortgaging her home, she found out that the deal was not meant to be.

Before the order could be delivered, the head of the client's relocation department, who had not been involved in any of the client meetings with Laura, decided to cancel the order. In his mind, none of the employees had voiced complaints about relocating; therefore, dual-career family issues were not a problem. Laura was left with $350,000 in debt and no customer.

Although she was devastated, Laura's confidence in her ability to meet this dire situation motivated her to keep on going by finding another client to salvage her financial investment.

Laura then had the ingenious idea to target moving companies. She thought that her relocation counseling program would complement their existing moving-related services and would serve as a point of differentiation for the right company. Laura received a positive response from the head of marketing of one moving company. He was excited about the product as a premium for his moving clients and was prepared to order a thousand relocation kits—not as many as the first customer but enough to keep Laura and the fledgling company afloat and reduce her debt. He asked her to leave one of her program kits with him overnight so he could share her idea with his team. Against her better judgment, Laura left the kit with him confirming that she'd return in the morning for the kit and a signature on the contract. The next morning Laura was told that another person on the marketing team had already created a similar process, so there was no need for her product.

For most people, it would have seemed like another failure of another promising strategy, but not for Laura. She shared with the audience the philosophy she learned from her parents that kept her going after she was once again knocked down: failure is only feedback as to what you need to do differently.

Laura's keynote speech was intended to inspire self-confidence in the women in her audience. Her skill in telling the unvarnished true story of her false starts, precarious financial status, and eventual success earned her a standing ovation. I believe the audience was applauding not only Laura, but also the newly found sense of their own self-confidence that her speech inspired. By revealing her confidence in response to crisis story, Laura sparked the confidence of the women in the audience.

After hearing Laura's keynote speech, I sat down with her to learn more about how her confidence in crisis led to the eventual success of IMPACT Group:

KATHY: Where does your confidence come from?

LAURA: My mother always told me, "If you put your mind to it, you can do anything." She helped me prove her right in my quest to be an honor roll student, an award-winning basketball player, and a successful entrepreneur.

KATHY: How did you stay confident as you dealt with setbacks? What did you tell yourself that helped boost your confidence?

LAURA: I reminded myself constantly of the crying need for relocation services. I also relied on what I had learned as a state champion basketball player: go toward the goal. My father had drummed that basketball philosophy into me: always drive toward the basket! It is the only way to win! You can't worry about your competitor or who is getting in the way. Drive around them!

KATHY: Tell me more about how you created the strategy for your ultimate success.

LAURA: I never blamed anybody for my lost orders. Instead, I stepped back and noticed that I had already gotten a yes from two business leaders. It was other people who had put the kibosh on the deal. That fact boosted my confidence.

I then thought of my winning strategy. What if I could tell the story of a real family—mother, father, preteen son, and six-year old-daughter—who had experienced the personal trauma of relocation? And what if I used my skill as a speaker to convey that story to a large audience of business professionals so they could see the need as I did?

I created a slideshow that depicted the tears of the six-year-old as she packed up her teddy bear; the sadness of the twelve-year-old boy sitting on the steps hugging his best friend goodbye; the sense of loss as the family waved goodbye to neighbors. With each slide, I told a story of lost friends and lost comfort zones. It was that story that dramatized the need.

KATHY: Was your confident attitude contagious during the setbacks and eventual victory?

LAURA: My business partner and husband, Mike, told me he never doubted we would be successful because I never doubted we would. I always believed there was a path forward. I just had to find it. We just had to keep experimenting until we found the right path.

And finally, the conference keynote opportunity came up and I could tell my real family story. Many people in the audience reached out to me after I spoke to inquire about our relocation solutions. Two weeks later, I had orders for more than a thousand program kits. Our relocation business has been growing ever since. I know firsthand from my work that confidence is the bedrock of creativity.

How else would you find a way to keep going in the face of adversity? Think about what you can take away from Laura's story about how to be confident in response to the crises that come your way. Here are just a few of the key lessons I learned:

- Keep focused on your ultimate goal and your mighty cause.
- Surround yourself with people who believe in you.
- Do not blame the people who set up roadblocks.
- Move into action. Experiment until you find the right path.
- Play to your strengths to find the winning strategy that resolves the crisis.
- Believe in yourself. Remember how your confidence in past crises served you well.

Being Curious in Response to Conflict

I am constantly on the lookout for people who exude the quality of being curious in the face of disagreement. Business leaders encounter pushback from all sides. Maybe there is an investor, or a board member, or a peer, or a direct report, or even a whole segment of the employee population or customer base who does not agree with your position on a key issue. I believe the best asset-based thinking (ABT) strategy in response to conflicting points of view is to be curious enough to find out why people oppose you.

Frances Kissing, the leader of the Catholics for Choice movement, has been part of the contentious abortion rights debate that has polarized people in the United States for the past thirty years. I know of no other issue that divides people so intensely and so rapidly.

On January 20, 2011, Kissling was interviewed for the American Public Media radio program, *On Being*.[1] In that interview, she shared her approach to finding commonality—not common ground—with pro-life advocates. Commonality is about getting to a place where opposing parties understand where each other is coming from. In contrast, common ground is about finding areas of agreement. With as heated an issue as abortion, common ground is unlikely and maybe even impossible in some cases. Commonality, however, is almost always an achievable goal. All it takes is a little curiosity.

In the interview, Kissling explained that mutual trust and respect come out of conversations aimed at learning more about the values of those with conflicting points of view. In contrast, the pressure of finding common ground, of coming to an agreement with her pro-life opponents, works against their understanding of each other. The first step, she said, is to be genuinely interested and curious enough about your opponent's point of view that you establish a certain level of trust. Trust then leads to a true sense of the commonality we share as human beings. As she mentions in the interview, the hallmark of a civil debate is when you can acknowledge the good in another's positions, values, and concerns. The goal is to honor others' values without giving up your own.

I have seen curiosity in the face of conflict resolve major disagreements. Curiosity sows the seeds of trust and creates opportunities to see value in somebody else's points. When conflicting parties trust and can see the value in each other's positions, the bar to finding a way out of the conflict altogether is significantly lowered.

Think of what happens in matrixed organizations when people disagree. When you operate in a matrix, people may have different managers for the different projects they are involved in and there is often no final authority. In such cases, decisions are the result of influence through advocacy and inquiry. The Kissling strategy of learning why others believe as they do is an example of influence through inquiry. Inquiry requires curiosity as a quality of being. This curiosity fosters genuine interest in and understanding of the people on the other side of the issue. It also generates goodwill and trust between the two sides.

The Rule of Three

The rule of three is an ABT strategy to increase one's influence through curiosity. I have seen this tool build trust between people who on the surface seemed miles apart on issues. It is especially useful for leaders tasked with managing resistance to change. The rule of three involves asking the opposing party the following three questions and really listening to their answers:

- Why is this so important to you?
- Can you tell me more about why this is so important to you?
- Please tell me even more about why your position is so important to you.

The goal here is to not sound as if you are cross-examining the person with opposing views. Rather, I am suggesting you inquire with genuine curiosity so you can learn about the person's deeper values and concerns. Try using the Rule of Three in minor disagreements to develop your quality of being curious in response to conflict.

When Both Sides Lose

When two parties are not the least bit curious about the other person's whys, a stalemate occurs. Other people are pulled in to settle the issue and, as a result, one side loses. Sometimes both sides lose. Now imagine this scenario.

John, who works in human resources as an organizational development strategist, is asked to lead the company's organizational restructuring. He assembles a cross-functional team to lead the redesign process, and they conduct a thorough assessment of the current and future state of the organization involving key stakeholders in the assessment. Now it is recommendation time, when the influence effort is most critical and most vulnerable.

John believes his recommendations are rock solid. He has thoroughly investigated the options and vetted them with all with key stakeholders save two—the CEO, Elizabeth, and the HR director, Matt. To John's surprise, Elizabeth voices strong concerns about the viability of the new organizational structure. When John reacts by advocating for his findings, he comes across as defensive and closed-minded. Then Matt chimes in in agreement with Elizabeth, which makes John even more defensive. He feels betrayed that Matt has joined forces with Elizabeth instead of him. The conversation devolves into a war of words, and eventually John is taken off the project. Not only are his recommendations ignored, he loses credibility as a trusted advisor in the company.

Think about the direction the conversation could have gone in if John had attempted to influence through inquiry as opposed to advocacy. What would he have gained, and how different would the outcome have been if he had been curious about the reasons behind Elizabeth's and Matt's concerns? What if John had used the rule of three strategy?

By being curious in response to conflict, John could have changed the nature of the conversation from finding agreement to discovering commonality on the level of values and concerns. He may have found a way to address Elizabeth's concerns within the context of his recommendations. He certainly would have earned their trust and increased his own credibility.

Being Courageous in Response to Challenges

Margaret Thatcher, the longest-serving British prime minister of the twentieth century and the only woman to have held that office, died on April 4, 2013, as I was writing this chapter. Her death led me to reflect on her "Iron Lady" moniker, the qualities of being it referenced, and her signature presence as a leader.

The Soviet army newspaper *Red Star* first used the "Iron Lady" tag after Thatcher's famous speech on January 19, 1976, "Britain Awake."[2] In that speech she railed against the Labour Party for "dismantling" British defenses against Russia, a country that she said was "bent on world domination" and "acquiring the means to become the most powerful imperial nation the world has ever seen." It is not so difficult to see why the newspaper dubbed her the "Iron Lady" after that jarring speech. But why did that nickname stick with friends as well as foes well into Thatcher's retirement years? Her foes (and there were many) used it pejoratively. Her friends (and there were also many) used it admiringly.

I believe the nickname stuck because Margaret Thatcher showed the world time after time, for nearly forty years, that she was a leader who had the courage of her convictions when facing her most challenging goals. Whether you agreed with her stand or not did not matter. People on all sides of every issue experienced Thatcher as steadfast, determined, and courageous. That is what this third quality of being is all about.

While the nature of the challenge may differ significantly for those in the political versus business landscape, the quality of being courageous is universally beneficial. Here are two sets of opposing qualities that apply to any set of challenging goals.

Being Courageous
- Making a tough decision and standing by it
- Admitting when things are not okay
- Asking others to do what's difficult
- Being able to stand alone
- Staying the course

Being Fearful
- Saying, "I'll think about it," when a decision has already been made
- Pretending everything is okay
- Hesitating to make difficult requests
- Seeking approval
- Changing direction too soon or too often

I am certain you can add items to these lists based on your personal experiences of responding to challenging goals. The point here is to decide which qualities of being you most want to display, given your specific circumstances.

Being Courageous During a Divestiture

There are three major challenges in the process of being spun off: you must cooperate with prospective buyers during the due diligence period, continue to run a solid business operation, and spearhead an effective transition.

David, the head of a large industrial manufacturing business, was dealing with the third challenge of the divestiture process, ensuring an effective transition. He decided that he wanted to be courageous in "admitting when things are not okay." He knew the transition would be difficult on many fronts: integrating new processes, adopting a new identity, and learning the norms of a new culture, to name just a few. Based on his analysis of the qualities of being he wanted to display, David outlined exactly what he was struggling with to his executive team. He invited the team to do the same, and they ended up facilitating an open forum meeting for the whole company that they called Struggles and Solutions. The response from all levels of the organization was amazing. Employees had been craving the forthright admission of struggles and were excited about creating practical solutions.

This is just one example of how being courageous in response to challenging goals can strengthen your leadership and the performance of your organization. Take this moment to reflect on your goals. Identify at least one way of being courageous in the face of the challenges in your path. Work on demonstrating that quality for one week. Then select another the following week, and then another for the week after that. Being courageous is your job as a leader for as long as you face challenges.

Recall, Remember, and Apply

The final ABT strategy for this chapter involves considering each quality of being that we have explored: confidence, curiosity, and courage. First, recall a time when you demonstrated each of those qualities in your role as a leader. Next, remember how you felt, what you said, and what you did. Finally, think about how you might apply that confidence, curiosity, or courage to a current situation you face. You may want to capture your reflections in a chart like table 11.1.

From Being to Doing

In chapter 10, I quoted Aristotle: "We are what we repeatedly do." Now I am going to take that thought and reverse it to capture what we have been exploring throughout this chapter: "We do what we repeatedly are." The qualities of being that comprise our signature presence are preliminary

Table 11.1   Recall, Remember, and Apply

How I Showed Up	Past		Present
	What Happened	What I Did in Response	How I Can Apply It
Confident in crisis			
Curious in conflict			
Courageous in challenge			

and fundamental to what we do as leaders. When you can intentionally call forth the qualities of being confident, curious, and courageous, they become launching pads for what you do as a highly effective ABT leader.

With this new awareness of your signature presence and this new knowledge of how to be a confident, curious, and courageous leader, you are ready to explore the leading positive change process and the seven key behaviors that make key moments matter and inspire people to follow in your footsteps.

12

Driving Positive Change

In the preceding chapters, we explored how to apply asset-based thinking (ABT) strategies to maximize your leadership effectiveness in the moment. In this chapter, we focus on what you must do to drive positive change over the long haul as you lead your team down the path of achieving a vision.

Change—positive or negative—can be provoked by crisis, chance, or choice (see figure 12.1). But, really, the source of change is irrelevant. It is what you do to lead your organization through the stages of change that makes the difference between success and failure and ensures that the change is positive and transformational. In the end, it all comes down to choice. Driving positive change is a matter of choosing to see whatever the provocation may be as a great opportunity to leap forward.

It is important for a leader to be intimately familiar with the stages of change that an organization undergoes in moving toward a vision. Each stage comes with a different emotional

Figure 12.1 The Stages of Transformational Change

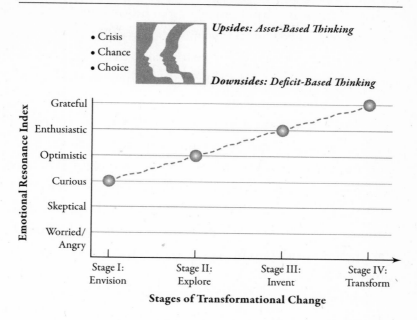

Stages of Transformational Change

resonance and requires different leadership behaviors in order to progress to the next one. Later in this chapter, I detail these behaviors and how they drive transformational change. For now, we'll focus on the goals and emotional targets for each stage to give you a panoramic view of the progression.

Notice that the initial provocation for transformative change can be crisis, chance, or choice. Your first leadership goal in the face of the provocation is to do whatever it takes to put yourself and your followers into the emotional zone of curiosity. This is shown in figure 12.1 as the first positive emotion on the emotional resonance index and corresponds with stage I of transformational change: envision. You cannot be curious if you are worried, angry, or even a bit skeptical about giving up the way things were for how they are going to be. Curiosity, as I discussed in chapter 11, is about taking a genuine interest in what is happening in order to find value in the situation. When you feel curious, you envision a new future worth living into. Curiosity is what it takes to get engaged. It opens the door to new realities, inspires hope, and paves the way for transformational change.

In stage II, the goal is to explore the new reality you want to create while you and the team ascend from curiosity into optimism. Optimism is a more motivating emotion, and it fuels exploration. A positive outlook about how things will turn out helps to put the new vision in focus. Optimism stimulates creativity and helps to clarify the journey and the end destination. Because you are optimistic, you trust that there will be paths forward.

In stage III, the goal is to begin inventing your new reality. Your optimism turns into full-on enthusiasm because you can see multiple paths forward; all you have to do is test them. You are experimenting and learning about what does or does not bring you closer to achieving your vision. You are enthusiastic about learning and pushing forward.

Stage IV is about completing the transformation into your new reality, looking back on all that has been accomplished, and feeling gratitude for the journey you have just completed and all you have learned along the way. In this final stage, you internalize and ratify the new behaviors and strategies that have led to your success.

The emotional journey of navigating the stages of transformational change can be experienced by an individual, a team, a whole organization, or even an entire city, as the next section shows.

Post-Katrina New Orleans: A Story of Transformational Change

After Hurricane Katrina decimated New Orleans in 2005, the Louisiana city was in dire straits. Over eighteen hundred people died in the storm, and the resulting flood and total property damage was estimated at $81 billion. To make matters worse, tens of thousands of jobs evaporated, taking with them billions in wages. The city's rise from the ashes of devastation in the years that followed truly captures how asset-based thinking and action on the parts of city leaders (elected and self-designated) can drive positive change.

Stage I: Envision

In an article in the *National Journal*, journalist Derek Thompson described three potential scenarios for New Orleans in the aftermath of the great hurricane:

> *Scenario 1:* "New Orleans slides into its own wet grave, another urban tragedy of geography and economics."

> *Scenario 2:* "New Orleans rebuilds itself as it was before—a sleepy southern belle of a town serving up wet weekends of intemperance."

> *Scenario 3:* "Hurricane Katrina somehow kick-starts an age of innovation and an economic renaissance in a city written off for dead."[1]

The Big Easy chose the third path. A core group of leaders made up of residents and business owners took it upon themselves to get curious about what positive change could come out this crisis. They envisioned a new future for the city as the technology mecca of the South.

Stage II: Explore

Thompson's article chronicled how entrepreneurs like Kenneth Purcell, founder of Iseatz, a service that lets shoppers book multiple travel arrangements on one website, migrated back to New Orleans to explore ways of making this vision of New Orleans as an innovation hub come true. In fact, the pending revival of the city was driven by the optimism of what Thompson called the "New Orleans boomerang generation," a group of proud reformers whose confidence in the merits of their hometown led them back in droves to start up new businesses.

As part of New Orleans's effort to rebuild itself after the natural disaster, city leaders explored ways to market the city to the wider US population as a destination for start-ups. Leaders found a number of benefits to promote, such as the much lower costs of living, labor, and office space in New Orleans compared to leading high-tech cities, such as San Francisco, Seattle, and New York.

Stage III: Invent

With many boomerangers returning home to set up shop, the path to achieving New Orleans's vision of regeneration was becoming clear—and exciting. This enthusiasm for the progress that had been made and the possibility of what could come next drove self-appointed leaders to invent a culture that would support the vision. These leaders created a nonprofit called the

Idea Village aimed at supporting entrepreneurial talent in New Orleans by connecting local and national partners and providing educational and networking opportunities.

Stage IV: Transform

In the past couple of years, New Orleans has been basking in the glow of its successful transformation from its post-Katrina slump. In 2011, the *Wall Street Journal* named it the "most improved" city for business, emphasizing its "pro-growth attitude."[2] In 2012, *Time* magazine called the city a "hub for incubating new businesses," and cited its "new culture of entrepreneurship" as one of the reasons for its revival.[3] Just imagine the gratitude the boomerang gang and other city leaders feel as they step back to take stock of these objectively positive assessments of their efforts. My hope is that they are taking stock and learning from their successes.

The Seven Key Dos of Positive Change

Highly effective leaders behave in certain, specific ways as they move through the progressive stages of change. I developed table 12.1 to help you understand the important "dos"— behaviors at each stage and what you want your followers to feel and do as a result. As we go through each stage, I will use the example of CEO Wendy Leebov, who has been transforming her company, Language of Caring (formerly Leebov Golde Group), from an on-site training and organizational change company to a cultural transformation company featuring web-based learning systems and on-site implementation services.

Table 12.1   What Highly Effective Leaders Do: The Seven Key Behaviors for Transformational Change

	Stage I: Envision	Stage II: Explore	Stage III: Invent	Stage IV: Transform
Key behaviors	1. Respond (don't react) 2. Act as if . . .	3. Shape the new path forward	4. Invent new ways of operating 5. Show fierce resolve 6. Bounce back	7. Celebrate and learn
Impact on followers	They feel curious. They embrace and expand on the vision.	They feel optimistic. They follow the new path forward.	They feel enthusiastic. They create new ways of operating and make course corrections.	They feel grateful. They achieve the vision.

Stage I: Envision

In stage I of an episode of transformational change, highly effective leaders must *respond, not react* (key leadership behavior 1) to whatever has initiated the process of change—crisis, chance, or choice. As I discussed in chapter 10, being responsive is about taking the time to digest what is happening. By reflecting on the prevailing winds of change, leaders can get a glimpse of what might be possible. As they step back and take stock, they can choose the response that creates energy and stimulates the curiosity of their followers so that they too can embrace the change.

Wendy Leebov and her team recognized that the demand for increasing patient satisfaction in hospitals was rising, largely due to new health care regulations. Wendy explained to me that in 2012, 30 percent of Medicare reimbursements became tied to patient experience scores as measured by the Hospital Consumer Assessment of Healthcare Providers and Systems (HCAHPS) survey, the first national standardized, publicly reported survey of patients' perspectives on hospital care. It was around that time that Wendy had also been thinking about capitalizing on her reputation as a trusted consultant and advisor in the health care industry. Furthermore, the digital world of distance learning was exploding. Wendy began to envision a new business model that would allow her to deliver her services in a way that would satisfy the escalating demand, while leveraging her reputation and the available technology. The potential for scaling her business using a video learning system seemed to be within reach. By reflecting on and responding to the converging opportunities around her, Wendy found her chance to drive positive change.

Key leadership behavior 2, *acting as if*, requires that you take actions that indicate the vision is already happening in small, but important, ways. For example, you might develop a business plan based on what you intend to do, or you might hire a person with subject matter expertise who is essential to achieving the vision, or you might purchase equipment and software to meet your future infrastructure needs. Such actions signal that you are serious and committed to creating a new and better future.

Wendy conducted visioning sessions with her team and invested in creating the Language of Caring—a video-based skill-building system, support materials, and on-site services to help health care employees master and apply the communication skills key to excellent patient outcomes, staff satisfaction, and elevated HCAHPS performance. Her leadership actions helped pique curiosity among her team members about the potential benefits of the new vision. As her team joined forces with Wendy, they began to own and embrace the new vision. On a much broader scale, Wendy saw that the new Medicare legislation had expedited what she called the patient experience movement, which galvanized millions of health care professionals worldwide to create a kind of tipping point in favor of improving the patient experience. Wendy and her team immediately saw the movement as evidence that their new vision for growth was meeting an existing aspiration within her client base.

Stage II: Explore

As optimism and ownership builds, the leader's next task is to *shape the new path forward* (key leadership behavior 3). This requires giving yourself and your team the space and time to generate the robust strategies and the specific behaviors that will secure the desired future. For example, the leader can work with a small team to generate a straw model of the new strategies and new behaviors that are required to drive positive change. Then that model can be cascaded throughout the organization with each level expanding on the details of the vision. Eventually everyone has a clear picture of the new future. What is more, they have contributed to that picture, which increases their ownership and commitment to making it a reality.

Wendy and her four-person leadership team collaborated to explore the new strategies they had identified to drive their business transformation:

- Changing the name of the company to "Language of Caring"
- Building a web-based learning system infrastructure
- Marketing a new service platform
- Building a web and social media presence

Notice that each of the strategies required new behaviors. For example, Wendy, as CEO, had to learn how to create compelling video messages and implementation services that inspire and teach her clients as much as her live appearances do and that produce comparable or better results. The sales force had to shift their focus to marketing new services with different features and benefits. They also had to expand their target markets to diverse types of health care organizations seeking improvement solutions. The training team had to work with each client organization's in-house facilitators and teach them how to effectively use the video learning system. The key lesson here is that exploring new strategies and behaviors should touch every level and role in an organization. The leaders must create a cascading process that helps each employee find the ways he or she can contribute to realizing the new vision.

Stage III: Invent

With new behaviors and strategies in hand and your enthusiasm building, you and your team will begin to *invent new ways of operating* that bring you closer to your vision (key leadership behavior 4).

Remember that you (and perhaps your direct reports) will always be ahead of the rest of the organization. While you are inventing, others may still be exploring what the new vision calls for. It is common at this stage to continually reinvent processes to find what works best. You may find that the organization as a whole is lacking the necessary skills and competencies to achieve the vision. That may mean hiring or outsourcing the right expertise and restructuring roles and responsibilities. Leading such an effort requires that you show *fierce resolve* (key leadership behavior 5) and commitment to your vision.

Adapting to new ways of operating can be difficult, even when the vision is well embraced. People may want to shift, but they often need to imitate the behavior of their leaders to do so. Sticking with the objective is the role of the leader, no matter how difficult the barriers or the resistance may be. Your team will be watching you for any sign of wavering. It is human nature for followers to test the resolve of their leaders. That is why you must be bold in showing your commitment by taking decisive actions such as these:

- Recognizing failed strategies
- Being positive and proactive in the face of small failures along the way
- Experimenting with new ways of operating to figure out what works best
- Finding strategic partners to invest in the new vision

Behaviors that *show fierce resolve* are cousins of behaviors that show your ability to *bounce back* (key leadership behavior 6). By stage III of driving positive change, you can be certain of encountering situations that are potentially mentally and emotionally devastating and have the power to jeopardize the success of your transformation. Bouncing back is about regaining your equilibrium and showing up with at least as much enthusiasm and energy after confronting a major setback or disappointment as you had in the very beginning.

Once again, people will be examining how well you respond to these potentially damaging circumstances. Leaders have a tremendous amount of responsibility to demonstrate that they can and will bounce back. What you do will be contagious—for better or worse. What is more, your resilience will give your team a reason to trust your leadership—to trust that you have what it takes to prevail over barriers large and small.

Think about moments in your past as a leader when you have been able to bounce back. Zone in on what you did to demonstrate your resilience. Reminding yourself of the concrete actions you took will give you the strength and determination to once again bounce back the next time the circumstances require it.

Use the following four ABT steps to refresh your memory about when and how you have been able to bounce back and regain lost ground. To illustrate how the steps work, I use an example from my own experience as the leader of a consulting and coaching company:

Step 1: Describe the setback: "A Fortune 100 client canceled a $350,000 contract because of a budget crisis. We had already staffed the project and booked the revenue in our budget."

Step 2: Describe your initial feelings and thoughts about the setback using the see-feel-think awareness tool:

- "I saw a gigantic revenue hole."
- "I felt totally blindsided, but at the same time, I was empathetic with our client contact. I could see she really hated being the bearer of bad news."
- "I asked myself: *How are we going to dig ourselves out of this hole?*"

Step 3: Describe how you bounced back—what you said, saw, and did:

- "My team and I saw the need to connect to our client during their economic downturn."
- "We said that we would agree to cancel the engagement with no financial penalties."

- "We invited our client contact to the free seminars that we now had time to offer to existing and prospective clients."

Step 4: Describe how you gained lost ground: "We used our downtime from the canceled contract to market to new clients while cutting our expenses to the bone. It took three months for us to bounce back, to get out of the red. But that setback experience has served us well. We now have a much more diversified client base with more reliable cash flow. And even more important, we know just how resilient we can be and that is a source of great pride."

I often remind myself of how we bounced back in the past when we face setback experiences now. Being resilient enough to bounce back is how we see ourselves as a company. (I recommend jotting down your notes first and then telling the story to a committed listener so that the memory solidifies itself in your long-term memory.)

When it came to inventing new ways of operating, Wendy soon realized she did not have enough staff to meet the growing demand for services to improve the patient experience. One of her first actions was to take on a business partner, Jill Golde, to serve as co-owner and senior vice president of client experience. With the support of Chaim Bank as head of marketing and Nikki Gollub Bank as writer and editor, Wendy and Jill were able to divide the customer base in two in order to handle the myriad requests for briefings and demos of the new video training program and to serve more clients without sacrificing further development.

As the market and the company's client base expanded, Wendy and Jill added a third partner, Dorothy Sisneros, and the three quickly added a CEO, a vice president of physician services, a web developer, and an extended team of associate subcontractors trained to partner with and support clients. Wendy, Jill, and Dorothy have restructured roles time and again to accommodate growth and ensure an aggressive sales strategy, marketing through social media and webinars, and new product development. In addition, Wendy continues to work with long-time colleagues and customers to fine-tune the group's products and services, ensure quality and results, and stay alert to emerging trends and needs.

I asked Jill if she had ever seen Wendy demonstrate fierce resolve. Jill responded without hesitation: "Every time Wendy speaks about the quality patient experience, you can see how committed she is to changing the whole culture of care. This is a real mission for Wendy, not just a thriving business. I think Wendy's fierce resolve to change the way patients and their families experience the health care they receive has rubbed off on me and our whole team. We are on a mission now too, and we believe that we will achieve the transformation."

Stage IV: Transform

This final stage in the transformation process is the one that yields results: the vision has been achieved. In most transformations, the primary metrics of success are financial, operational, customer-centric, and cultural. But highly effective leaders should not just let the metrics speak for themselves. Instead, they must find ways of drawing attention to the victories and leaps forward by *celebrating and learning* (key leadership behavior 7). Praising the individual and collective efforts in a specific and detailed way leads to learning about the key drivers of a particular success. We learn best if we take the time to deconstruct what happened. Then those lessons learned can be repeated over and over again.

As you celebrate and learn from your success, you and your team will automatically shift to a place of gratitude, the most rewarding of all the positive emotions because it acknowledges a major victory with humility. When you feel grateful, you realize that you have had the wind behind your back in the form of a little luck and a lot of support from others. As a leader, feeling and showing gratitude to others helps to build trust, form lasting relationships, and inspire admiration.

Although the transformation of Wendy Leebov's business is not yet complete, the early signs of success are clearly apparent. The firm's customer base has grown from twelve to sixty-five participating hospitals in two years. Her program impact scores have been highly correlated with significant improvements in HCAHPS patient survey scores. Through her new webinars and online blog, Wendy has increased her community of followers from none in 2011 to six thousand in 2013.

I asked Wendy if she and her team celebrated and learned from their successes. She paused for a moment and then said, "I've never learned so much, so fast in my whole career. This new business model is working so well, I almost have to pinch myself to remember it's real. My partners and I are so grateful for our strategic relationships, for our long-term clients and our new ones, and for the changes in health care regulations that are fueling our success. We often just find ourselves speechless! And above all, we are excited to see heartwarming improvements in the experiences patients and their families have at the hands of (or mercy of) health care organizations."

When you achieve your vision, you are on top of the world. You know you have worked tirelessly and will continue to do so to sustain the transformation. Transformations always need to be tweaked. And then one day you will be back to stage I for another amazing transformational journey.

We have almost arrived at the conclusion of *Lead Positive*. In the next and last chapter, I map out how all of the ABT strategies you have learned in the course of this book work together to help you as a leader move through the four stages of transformational change (as you will see, this process parallels the Hero's Journey we discussed in chapter 7). We come full circle in the next chapter as we explore how the See-Say-Do framework can help you drive positive change.

13

The Asset-Based Leadership Advantage

Driving positive change in all that you see, say, and do is the true asset-based leadership advantage. Remember, asset-based thinking (ABT) means you look at yourself and the world through the eyes of what is working, what strengths are present, and what the potentials are. This is what is required of leaders as they cascade positive change throughout an organization and inspire others toward achieving a shared vision. This last chapter is about how the Lead Positive See-Say-Do framework applies to every stage of the transformational change process.

Table 13.1 shows how just a few of the tools you have learned in this book for what highly effective leaders see and say can form the basis for the seven key leadership dos that drive positive change.

Using the example of the DuPont Company, which we first encountered in part 1, I will illustrate how an ABT mind-set

Table 13.1 What Highly Effective Leaders See, Say, and Do to Drive Transformational Change

What Highly Effective Leaders . . .	Stage I: Envision	Stage II: Explore	Stage III: Invent	Stage IV: Transform
See	The third way See and seize kairos moments What do you want? What do you need?	Who is on your Mount Rushmore?	The ASA (acknowledge–scan–act) shift	Remember your collective success
Say	Say it with substance, sizzle, and soul	Show your skin in the game	Positive provocations	Chronicle and communicate your collective Hero's Journey
Do	Respond (don't react) Act as if . . .	Shape the new path forward	Invent new ways of operating Show fierce resolve	Celebrate and learn

and the see, say, and do tools can work together to form a comprehensive framework for effective leadership and drive positive change through every stage of the process. Recall that the DuPont Company's transformational change process involved its transition from primarily a chemical company into a "dynamic science company, creating sustainable solutions essential to a better, safer, healthier life for people everywhere."[1]

Stage I: Envision

See

At the beginning of the process of transformational change, highly effective leaders rise above the situation to create a *third way* of seeing what is in front of them. As we discussed in chapter 1, seeing a third way is about stepping outside the binary good-bad continuum. This entirely outside perspective helps you to redefine the situation and get out of whatever the bind may be.

While DuPont was transforming the vision and strategies for the company as a whole, a number of smaller functional and business transformations were happening simultaneously, including the transformation of corporate marketing and sales. Mark Wagner, corporate sales officer, and Tim Carmack, commercial excellence manager for the Americas, were at the helm of this effort. As their first step, Mark and Tim assumed a reflective stance so they could find a third way of seeing what needed to be done. By rising above the current reality, they realized that the function did not just need to be tweaked; it needed to be reinvented.

To meet the demands of the global marketplace and the sales environment, more challenging than ever before, Mark and Tim envisioned a series of sequential training and development experiences they called the Talent Management Journey. The Talent Management Journey was designed to provide DuPont sales professionals with the knowledge, attitudes, and skills they needed for success in the new, more demanding business environment. For example, Mark and Tim knew that salespeople needed to move beyond a conventional sales mind-set into a wider commercial mind-set. Salespeople needed to learn to think like marketers in order to communicate the total value proposition and speak from the point of view of what is best for the customer, not just for DuPont.

When it came to cultivating new attitudes, Mark and Tim realized that their sales teams needed to shift into a more resilient, optimistic, and confident mode to face the challenge of selling in the midst of an economic downturn. I worked with them on a set of ABT tools to satisfy this requirement. In order to reinvent the third ingredient, skills, Mark and Tim commissioned research to identify the skill profile of the most successful sales professionals at DuPont. This research yielded the skill set of what is now referred to as the sales innovator. Now the teams had a way to assess their individual strengths and areas for improvement relative to the sales innovator success profile.

By stepping outside the confines of conventional thinking, leaders also open themselves to *seeing and seizing kairos opportunities* in order to create kairos moments—those moments of clarity, ripe with possibility, when opportunity and action intersect (chapter 3).

From their third-way vantage point, Mark and Tim could easily see the *kairos* opportunity: not only were they itching to overhaul the entire corporate sales function, they could see the readiness of the sales teams for transforming the type of development and support that corporate sales had been offering into more relevant, accessible, and systematic approaches.

A huge objective of leadership is creating connections and buy-in to the vision. By asking those you lead what they want and what they need, you can see the way to hook your vision to their aspirations. Asking, *"What do you want?"* and *"What do you need?"* is about engendering goodwill and a collective enthusiasm toward achieving the new, shared vision (chapter 4).

Mark and Tim decided to take the collaborative approach to find out specifically what the sales teams wanted and needed in terms of new knowledge, attitudes, and skills to succeed in the new markets that DuPont was targeting. Almost all of the sales professionals they talked to said that they were vitally interested in learning how to be more resilient, optimistic, and confident. After learning new ways of staying positive, they would be primed for the new knowledge and skills they needed to acquire.

As a result of this feedback, Mark and Tim led sessions called "You ROC with Asset-Based Thinking" (ROC stands for resilience, optimism, and confidence). After offering You ROC for over eighteen months, the demand for the ABT sessions continues to escalate across all the DuPont businesses. By seeking the input of their teams, Mark and Tim were able to satisfy a growing need that served their interests and brought them closer to their vision of a new Corporate Sales function.

Say

When it comes to inspiring others to commit to the vision, leaders can rely on the lead positive communication road map that I first discussed in chapter 5. I often suggest that leaders engage a wide, cross-functional swath of the organization gathered in groups of ten to fifteen people at a time to listen and then craft their own versions of what they want to say in stage I. As team members share their responses within and outside these groups, they socialize and spread the what and the why of the vision throughout the organization. But more important, the way they respond to the sizzle section (the how) helps to surface new ideas and themes that leaders can distill into new strategic approaches.

Tim and I worked on a succinct *substance, sizzle,* and *soul* message he could communicate to describe the transformation of corporate sales and explain how it would help drive sales success at DuPont as the company transformed itself. Tim crafted the initial part of his message by going back and forth between the elements of substance (the what) and soul (the why). Next, he added the element of sizzle to describe the how—how corporate sales support would actually work to serve the needs of all sales professionals. Here is an outline of Tim's message:

Substance: The marketplace is changing. [Tim provided evidence of those changes, for example, globalization, sustainability imperatives, and austerity measures.]

Soul: DuPont is responding to those changes with a new vision: To be the world's most dynamic science company creating sustainable solutions essential to a better, safer, healthier life for people everywhere. One of the new strategies supporting this vision is addressing global challenges by "inclusive innovation," that is, by working together with more people in more places than ever to solve the food, energy, and protection needs of the world's growing population.

Substance: DuPont Corporate Sales is here to equip you with the knowledge, attitudes, and skills that are required for you to be successful in delivering DuPont's new vision and global collaborative solutions.

Soul: We want to serve you in new ways because we know you want to serve your customers in new ways.

Sizzle: Just as DuPont will be solving global challenges via "inclusive innovation," we will work together with you in the same spirit. We will set up a Global Sales Collaboratory to meet with more of our sales professionals in more places than ever to provide the innovative sales solutions you need to meet your customers' emerging needs. [Tim went on to inspire the sales teams with stories of how the Talent Management Journey was already promoting sales success.]

Do

By taking the time to find a third way, see and seize the *kairos* opportunities, learn what followers need and want in order to succeed, and find the right words to tell the story of how you want to achieve, it becomes second nature for highly effective leaders to *respond (not react)* to leverage the positive forces at hand. And once you can see the positive potential hidden inside the transformative circumstances you face, then it is easy to *act as if* the vision is already happening.

By fully outlining the steps of their new integrated model, the Talent Management Journey, and how sales professionals would participate, Mark and Tim acted as if the achievement of their vision was a foregone conclusion. For more than two years, Mark, Tim, and their teams have been creating new *kairos* moments as they charge forward and have seen many new possibilities emerge. They both continue to cascade and expand their vision by involving key sales and marketing stakeholders in reshaping the vision and responding intentionally to the new circumstances that arise. In this way, they ensure that the vision remains fresh and engagement in the process is high.

Stage II: Explore

See

One of my favorite ABT exercises during this exploratory stage of driving positive change is *Who is on my Mount Rushmore?* (chapter 4) because it allows you to identify people within or outside your organization who already behave in ways that advance the new vision. This exercise first requires you to consider four people you admire and why. The second part is contacting those people and asking them how they do what they do. Invariably, their answers yield valuable lessons for cultivating that behavior across your organization.

Mark wanted to make sure that sales managers could be effective coaches and leaders for their sales team members; he also saw the coach and leader roles as moving beyond mere sales support. He felt that sales managers should be committed to helping each sales rep move to the next level of proficiency, which would require highly customized and personalized developmental coaching. And when it came to leadership behavior, Mark wanted sales managers to shift from a boss-subordinate dynamic into becoming true sources of inspiration for each person and for their sales teams as a whole.

Mark turned to author and speaker John Maxwell, one of the professionals he had nominated to be on his Mount Rushmore, for advice and counsel. Maxwell felt that the last two levels in his system, "The 5 Levels of Leadership," would offer a template for creating the coaching and leadership competencies Mark was looking for in sales managers across DuPont.[2] Maxwell defines level 4 leadership as people development: people follow because of what you have done for them personally. Level 5 leadership, pinnacle, is about people following you because of who you are and what you represent.

Mark brought Maxwell in as a keynote speaker to introduce the concepts of level 4 and 5 leadership at the DuPont sales summit in 2012. In 2013, he extended this work by creating his own seminar based on Maxwell's leadership principles, adding his own takes on the specific behaviors he believed would help DuPont sales managers to become consummate coaches and inspiring leaders.

Say

As a leader, *showing your skin in the game* at this stage is necessary to maintain progress and engagement. By exposing your vulnerability and voicing why you personally believe in the new vision you are working together to make a reality, you inspire your team to make their own personal commitments.

In the early stages of introducing the Talent Management Journey concepts and methods to sales organizations across DuPont, Mark and Tim scheduled briefings with dozens of sales teams to connect with them and explain in person the reasons behind the transformation and their commitment to its success. This was their way of showing their personal skin in the game. Instead of sending a digital brochure announcement, they took the time to show up in person to promote the new process, answer questions, and invite people to sample the new offerings firsthand. An added bonus was that this personal approach allowed them to identify early adopters to help launch the new process.

Do

As we discussed in the previous chapter, *shaping the new path forward* is about exploring the specific strategies and behaviors necessary to realize the vision. As the leader, your responsibility is to engage the entire organization in this step. Not only will input from each level of the organization help to solidify what exactly needs to be done next, it gives each person a sense of ownership and ensures everyone has a clear picture of the new direction.

Mark and Tim presented their sales teams with a vividly illustrated map of the Talent Management Journey that detailed the various paths they could travel as they increased their sales skills and deepened their sales competency—for example:

- How to be a successful negotiator
- How to become more resilient, optimistic, and confident with ABT
- How to coach and lead more effectively

As participation in the Talent Management Journey grew, so did the positive reputation of this new, more systematic, input-driven, and experiential approach to learning. Within the first year, Mark, Tim, and the rest of their team knew that they had hit a home run: demand was outstripping their capacity to deliver. Their new approach, which allowed salespeople to choose their own paths toward skill development, had become a new path forward.

Stage III: Invent

See

Of course, nothing ever works out exactly as planned. And when this (inevitably) happens, it is easy to feel disappointed and disheartened. To disrupt a negative downward spiral and discover the hidden assets in the situation, you can use the *ASA (acknowledge-scan-act) shift* exercise from chapter 1. By acknowledging the negative, scanning for ways you can benefit from the setback, and acting in new ways to realize that possible benefit, you ensure you and your team stay on track to realizing the vision.

The ASA shift came in handy for Tim and me the day we found out that my book, *Change the Way You See Everything*, an essential part of the learning package for the Talent Management Journey, would soon be out of print. We panicked at the prospect of not having the book to support the learning process—and then we turned to the ASA shift. We *acknowledged* how anxious we felt about the situation and then *scanned* for possible remedies and new opportunities. It was then that I remembered my editor had invited me to call her if I ever needed help. I moved into *action* immediately by calling her, and she helped me negotiate with the publisher for a fast turnaround second printing. Not only were Tim and I relieved; averting the near setback helped bring us closer and strengthen our working relationship.

Say

Building on the positive effects of the ASA shift, the *positive provocations* tool (chapter 4) helps to get your team excited about the possibilities of the future and develop creative new strategies to move toward the vision. Positive provocations usually begin, "I wonder what would happen if . . . ," and call for a positive answer to the question.

To find a creative solution to the growing demand for the Talent Management Journey program that was outstripping capacity, Tim asked himself and the corporate sales team, "I wonder what would happen if we asked for volunteers to become certified trainers for the most popular talent management courses?" The response to Tim's provocation proved to be highly positive. A handful of people from the marketing and sales functions volunteered to be considered for certification. As a result, corporate sales was able to begin the certification process immediately.

The positive provocations leadership tool invites people to wonder about expanding the repertoire of how they make valuable contributions to the company. Tim struck a chord with a number of people who were interested in incorporating training into their existing sets of roles and responsibilities, which served his purpose of expanding the Talent Management Journey program while fulfilling the volunteers' need for new skill development.

Do

In stage III, leaders are transforming their own behavior. This leads to *inventing new ways of operating* with stakeholders inside and outside the organization. For Mark and Tim, this meant setting up rigorous evaluation and focus group processes with the sales managers and sales professionals they served. This new way of operating ensured that the programs they were offering remained highly relevant and evergreen. This inventive approach also ensured the highest participant satisfaction scores.

Situations change, behaviors change, and ways of operating change. Throughout it all, it is important for the leader and his commitment to the vision to remain unchanged. By showing your *fierce resolve*, you make it clear that your belief in the vision has not wavered. And you inspire your team to follow your lead. Tim showed his fierce resolve to achieving his vision for the Talent Management Journey by continuing to lead teams and manage the development of others after new responsibilities took him in different directions. To illustrate Tim's commitment, he ensured that his next assignment at DuPont allowed him to continue delivering ABT seminars.

Stage IV: Transform

See and Say

Once the vision has been realized, taking the time to *remember your collective success* is vital. Moving a step back to view your progress through the lens of collaborative effort reinforces the merits of teamwork and the pride that comes from a job well done. Notice how the Hero's Journey from chapter 7 maps to each phase of the change process. In this case, everyone involved in moving the organization toward the vision is the Hero. After all, driving positive change requires heroic effort not only on the part of the leader but also on the part of those who follow. *Chronicling and communicating your collective Hero's Journey* is a way to create a permanent memory of your collective success that will live on in the hearts, minds, and souls of all those who contributed to the effort.

The first stage (envision) of driving transformational change naturally corresponds to the first step in the Hero's Journey: the Call. Leaders must be able to see the what and the why of their vision so they can feel inspired and inspire others. As you move through the second stage (explore) and attempt to engage more members of your organization, you will almost assuredly sense the Resistance to embracing the new vision. People will come up with all sorts of reasons not to pursue the vision. Your job as a leader is to listen respectfully to the pushback and work with it. Moving on regardless is what the next phase of the Hero's Journey, the Threshold Crossing, is all about. The Hero may still have concerns and anxiety, but decides to move forward anyway. This strong commitment bonds people together and elicits optimism so that you can continue on your Journey with the resilience to navigate the next stage.

The third stage (invent) is the Hero's longest, most trying (and at the same time, most rewarding) phase of the journey. There will be moments of true inspiration but also of abject despair as you face your Supreme Ordeal. But as you know by now, heroic adventures require that you work with whatever you encounter to firm up your resolve and march forward on to victory. In the fourth stage, the Return Home, with the boons and bounties of the journey (in this case, the bounty is the rewards associated with realizing the collective vision), is about ensuring that the valuable lessons learned along the way continue to transform the organization for the better.

Recently, I asked Mark and Tim some of the Hero's Journey questions as a way for them to mark how much they had accomplished and to describe the road map they had followed in achieving their vision. Here is what they said:

Step 1: The Call

KATHY: How did you come to realize the need for change?

MARK: I was a leader in one of DuPont's most customer-focused businesses for ten years. I know firsthand how critical sales and marketing skills are to growing and sustaining a business. When I took the job as VP of corporate sales, I had a line of sight into the sales organizations of every DuPont business. From the very start, the feedback we received told us it was time to reinvent the kind of support corporate sales had to offer. Everyone said it was time for a big change. That feedback told us we were ready.

Step 2: The Resistance

KATHY: When we first discussed using asset-based thinking to increase the resilience, optimism, and confidence of the DuPont Sales Force, you told me you thought ABT would be a "hard sell." How did you overcome the initial resistance?

TIM: It is true; initially some people were skeptical about whether a person could actually learn to change their attitudes. For example, many people in sales believe you are just "born" optimistic—you can't learn to become an optimist. Another big challenge was getting leadership to make the investment in time to develop their team's commercial skills. Sales leaders will unanimously agree that buying behaviors have changed over the past several years. However, not many make the connection between the changing behaviors of buyers with the need to continually develop the skill of the sales organization. One way we have found to overcome this is by starting the conversation with a few questions. For example, we ask, "Has medicine changed over the past several years?" When they inevitably answer yes, we follow up, "Well, would you want to go to a doctor who has never refreshed his or her skills?" The answer to that question is always, "Of course not," which greatly helps to make our case for the value of sales skill development.

Step 3: The Threshold Crossing

KATHY: Did the current work environment hold people back or block them from getting on board with your vision of the talent management journey?

MARK: The main barrier in getting people to commit to the journey was time—a lack of time. The shear workload for most sales managers and their reps keeps them off-the-charts busy. Eventually we overcame the time/busyness barrier by presenting seventy-five-minute overviews of our key programs to pique interest and stimulate enrollment. This strategy is what got us over the initial threshold and made the launch successful.

Step 4: The Journey

KATHY: There are always positive and negative forces at work in leading a transformative change process. How would you describe the five most positive forces you had working for you and what was the one biggest negative?

TIM: Our five positives were: (1) The sales professionals at DuPont are high achievers when it comes to upping their game. (2) The timing of the Talent Management Journey coincided with the transformation of DuPont into a global science company. (3) We had the profile of the sales innovator that gave people a research-based description of what it took to be successful in sales at DuPont. (4) The programs we created and updated matched the interests and needs of our audience. (5) We had a first-class leadership team in corporate sales that worked hard to coach and inspire the sales representatives and facilitate their progress through the program and inspire our participants.

Our biggest negative was that we were and are still stretched to the max in terms of meeting demand for the program—even with certifying people outside our department as trainers and facilitators. We have decided that the only way to scale our offerings is to adapt some of the programs to online platforms. We are experimenting with that right now.

Step 5: The Supreme Ordeal

KATHY: Tim, you called me one day and told me your travel budget had been put on hold as a cost-reduction measure. That meant you had to cancel some key engagements with your customers. Did that qualify as a "supreme ordeal"? How did you and your team overcome the negative impact of the travel freeze?

TIM: At first we were very apprehensive about the negative fallout from having to cancel on our customers. We saw the very real risks of losing ground and tarnishing our reputation for being reliable. But then we asked ourselves the ABT question, "How can we milk this problem for all it is worth?" Ultimately, after brainstorming the positive upsides that the travel freeze had to offer, we acted on the top five: (1) Share the travel freeze news ASAP with each customer and ask if they would consider letting us do some prework with the group by e-mail or teleconference. That way we would be even more prepared to deliver the programs when the freeze lifted. (2) Use the downtime to design and vet new programs we wanted to bring on board. (3) Use the downtime to evaluate and upgrade our website and e-learning platform. (4) Use the downtime to increase the number of motivational video blogs from Mark. (5) Use the downtime to interview people and gather success stories from our programs to highlight on the web and in person once the freeze was lifted.

Although three months of downtime was a "supreme ordeal" at the time, we managed to make the most of it. In fact, I think it actually brought us closer to some of our customers as a result.

Step 6: The Return Home

KATHY: Mark, how has creating the Talent Management Journey helped you to fulfill your mighty cause?

MARK: The whole creative process has helped me to leave behind a legacy of learning. I am always on the lookout for new techniques or methods that can help me excel as a leader and as a sales professional. The Talent Management Journey is a compilation of the best tools and principles we have available to everyone who wants to excel in sales. I look back on this assignment as one that has given me the chance to help the sales function of DuPont advance to the level of a true profession. I am very grateful that I had the opportunity to make such a worthwhile contribution.

Do

Once the signs of transformation begin to appear, leaders often feel such a profound internal sense of gratitude that they forget to celebrate out loud. After completing a Hero's Journey together, your team will want to celebrate your collective achievement—as a team. Publicly *celebrating your success* will instill a sense of team pride as well as ensure that each person feels valued for his or her individual effort. You almost can't do too much when it comes to praising effort. Keep the praise and the storytelling alive long enough to leave indelible posi-tive imprints on your culture and your leadership for years to come. There are countless stories to be told about the adven-ture. It is in the telling and retelling of those stories that people begin to recognize and feel grateful for the boons and bounties of the journey.

Mark and Tim made sure to follow up with individuals and teams after each *learning* experience. They asked for specific examples of how the new principles and practices from the Talent Management Journey were being put into action, such as evaluating situations using the five-to-one principles. Their follow-up process was timed in intervals of one week, three months, and six months. Next, they broadcast and celebrated the efforts people made to put their new learnings into practice. They communicated these stories formally on the DuPont website and through e-mail. And in any follow-up briefings and sessions, they made a point of recognizing the applications and giving proper credit to those who had earned it.

Scan-Snap-Savor

I hope this reflection on Mark and Tim's story has helped you to better plan and imagine how you can lead positive and drive your own transformational change using the See-Say-Do process. Note that table 13.1 calls out just a few of the ABT tools from the previous chapters. I encourage you to find the tools and strategies that resonate most with you and your leadership style and insert them into this framework. They can all play a role in helping you through the transformative change process.

There is one additional ABT strategy that I want to highlight because it is applicable to *every* stage of the change process. We first explored Scan-Snap-Savor in chapter 3. As you may recall, this exercise helps you to "take in the good" of the here-and-now so that you and those you lead are primed to see more of the positive dynamics occurring in the present moment:

- Scan for the positive facts happening in the present or immediate past.
- Snap a picture in your mind's camera of one of those positive facts complete with sensory details of the setting and your state of mind.
- Savor that image in your mind for thirty to sixty seconds, reliving the positive emotions associated with it.

I recommend you use Scan-Snap-Savor weekly as you and others lead the transformation effort. Remember to scan, snap, and savor the positive facts of your own effectiveness (self), the contributions of your team and members at every organizational level (others), and the circumstances that help you advance (situations). Being positive promotes proactive and creative effort, and this ABT strategy helps you and everyone else involved stay on the positive side of the emotional ledger.

Conclusion

Your Lead Positive Hero's Journey

I opened this book with a series of provocative propositions that I now want to pose to you personally.

What if you as a leader could:

See more possibilities than problems?

Say more about why and less about what and how?

Do the courageous thing instead of operating out of your comfort zone?

How much more effective would you be? How many more people would you inspire? How much better off would your organization and your community be today and in the long run?

This is what our Lead Positive adventure has been all about. I have introduced you to asset-based thinking (ABT) best practices and exemplary leaders to help you turn those what-ifs into your personal leadership reality. Your task now is to practice, practice, practice.

"We don't see things as they are, we see them as we are." This famous quote, widely attributed to author Anaïs Nin, was, is, and will forever be true.[1] But more than that, I believe that through ABT, we all have the power to make the things we see and who we are as leaders more positive and, ultimately, more effective.

Lead Positive is about giving you the language and the strategies you need to be confident in your own abilities. Then you can present yourself as a leader worthy of your followers' trust and commitment. You can leverage what you already know how to do—in the moment and over time—to:

- Be an authentic leader, aligned in all that you see, say, and do
- Be that base of positivity for your team and for your vision
- Be a source of inspiration for your followers
- Drive positive change

I hope that this book helps guide you on your own Lead Positive Hero's Journey.

Notes

Introduction

1. Burns, J. M. *Leadership*. New York: Harper Perennial Modern Classics, 2010.
2. Bass, B. M., and Avolio, B. J. "Transformational and Organizational Culture." *Public Administration Quarterly*, 1993, *17*(1), 112–121.
3. Paulson, T. L. *The Optimism Advantage: 50 Simple Truths to Transform Your Attitudes and Actions into Results*. Hoboken, NJ: Wiley, 2010.
4. Baumeister, R. F., Bratslavsky, E., and Finkenauer, C. "Bad Is Stronger Than Good." *Review of General Psychology*, 2001, *5*(4), 323–370.
5. Zull, J. E. *The Art of Changing the Brain: Enriching the Practice of Teaching by Exploring the Biology of Learning*. Sterling, VA: Stylus, 2002.
6. Cramer, K. D., and Wasiak, H. *Change the Way You See Everything*. Philadelphia, PA: Running Press, 2006.

Chapter 1

1. Grill-Spector, K., and Kanwisher, N. "Visual Recognition: As Soon as You Know It Is There, You Know What It Is." *Psychological Science*, 2005, *16*(2), 152–160.

2. CNN. "New York's Governor and Mayor of New York City Address Concerns of the Damage." September 2001. http://transcripts.cnn.com/TRANSCRIPTS/0109/11/bn.42.html.

3. Pooley, E. "Person of the Year 2001: Mayor of the World." December 2001. http://www.time.com/time/specials/packages/article/0,28804,2020227_2020306,00.html.

4. Hughes, R. L., Ginnett, R. C., and Curphy, G. J. *Leadership: Enhancing the Lessons of Experience.* New York: McGraw-Hill, 2006. Adapted with permission.

5. Brown, T. "Our Approach: Design Thinking." 2013. http://www.ideo.com/.

6. "Design Thinking Is Dead," panel discussion at DMI Design/Management Thinking 24 Conference, Portland, OR, June 2012.

7. Taylor, S. E. "Asymmetrical Efforts of Positive and Negative Events: The Mobilization of Minimization Hypothesis." *Psychological Bulletin,* 1991, *110*(1), 67–85.

8. Cooperrider, D. L., and Srivastva, S. "Appreciative Inquiry in Organizational Life." In W.P.R. Woodman (ed.), *Research in Organization Change and Development,* vol. 1. Greenwich, CT: JAI Press, 1987.

9. Hebb, D. O. *The Organization of Behavior.* New York: Wiley, 1949.

10. Doidge, N. *The Brain That Changes Itself: Stories of Personal Triumph from the Frontiers of Brain Science.* New York: Penguin, 2007.

11. Hanson, R., and Mendius, R. *Buddha's Brain: The Practical Neuroscience of Happiness, Love and Wisdom.* Oakland, CA: New Harbinger, 2009.

12. Hanson and Mendius. *Buddha's Brain.*

13. Taylor, S. E. "Asymmetrical Efforts of Positive and Negative Events: The Mobilization of Minimization Hypothesis." *Psychological Bulletin,* 1991, *110*(1), 67–85.

14. McGreevey, S. "Meditation's Positive Residual Effects." *Harvard Gazette,* November 13, 2012.

15. Bunker, K. A., and Webb, A. *Learning How to Learn from Experience: Impact of Stress and Coping.* Greensboro, NC: Center for Creative Leadership, 1992.

16. Powell, M. "In 9/11 Chaos, Giuliani Forged a Lasting Image." *New York Times*, September 21, 2007.

17. Hanson and Mendius. *Buddha's Brain.*

18. Gottman, J. M., and Notarius, C. I. "Decade Review: Observing Marital Interaction." *Journal of Marriage and Family*, 2000, *62*(4), 927–974.

19. Chaffin, E., and Cramer, K. *Leadership Series White Paper: A Case Study in Leadership Effectiveness, Cultural Cohesiveness, and Client Loyalty Among Seven Newly Acquired Companies*. March 2010.

20. CBS News. "Who Won the Presidential Debate? We Did." October 2012. http://www.cbsnews.com/video/watch/?id=7424666n.

21. The client's name has been changed to protect his privacy.

Chapter 2

1. DuPont. "Our Vision." 2010. http://www2.dupont.com/corp/en-us /our-company/vision.html.

2. McClelland, D. C., and Winter, D. G. *Motivating Economic Achievement*. New York: Free Press, 1969.

3. Encyclopaedia Britannica. "Gettysburg Address." November 1863. http:// www.britannica.com/EBchecked/topic/232225/Gettysburg-Address.

Chapter 3

1. Hanson, R. "Taking in the Good." IONS webinar and Wellspring Institute for Neuroscience and Contemplative Wisdom, Mar. 2012.

2. White, E. C. *Kaironomia: On the Will-to-Invent*. Ithaca, NY: Cornell University Press, 1987, p. 13.

3. White, *Kaironomia*.

Chapter 4

1. Bass, B. M., and Avolio, B. J. (eds.). *Improving Organizational Effectiveness Through Transformational Leadership*. Thousand Oaks, CA: Sage, 1994.

2. Cheer, J. F., and others. "Coordinated Accumbal Dopamine Release and Neural Activity Drive Good Directed Behavior." *Neuron*, 2007, *54*(2), 237–244.

3. Zimbardo, P., and Boyd, J. *The Time Paradox: The New Psychology of Time That Will Change Your Life*. New York: Simon & Schuster, 2008.

Chapter 5

1. Goleman, D. *Leadership and the Power of Emotional Intelligence*. Northhampton, MA: More Than Sound, 2011.
2. Lomax, A. "What Makes PepsiCo One of America's Best Companies." *Motley Fool*, February 27, 2013.
3. Useem, M. "America's Best Leaders: Indra Nooyi, PepsiCo CEO." *U.S. News & World Report*, Nov. 19, 2008.
4. Useem, "America's Best Leaders.
5. Ziobro, P. "PepsiCo Sales Indicate Turnaround Is Taking Hold." *Wall Street Journal*, February 14, 2013.
6. Birdwhistell, R. *Kinesics and Context*. Philadelphia: University of Pennsylvania Press, 1970.

Chapter 6

1. Churchill, W. "Their Finest Hour." June 1940. http://www .winstonchurchill.org/learn/speeches/speeches-of-winston-churchill /122-their-finest-hour.
2. Churchill, W. "Their Finest Hour." Audio. June 1940. http://www .youtube.com/watch?v=LsKDGM5KTBY.
3. Gladwell, M. *Outliers: The Story of Success*. New York: Hachette, 2008.
4. Gardner, J. W. *On Leadership*. New York: Free Press, 1990.

Chapter 7

1. "Secretariat—Belmont Stakes." Video. 1973. http://www.youtube.com /watch?v=xoFquax2F-k.
2. Secretariat Newsletter. "June 9,1973—Belmont Stakes—1½ Mile— Belmont Park." http://www.secretariat.com/past-performances /belmont/.
3. Nack, W. "Pure Heart." June 1990. http://sportsillustrated.cnn.com /vault/article/magazine/MAG1136808/1/index.htm.

4. Campbell, J. *The Hero with a Thousand Faces*. Novato, CA: New World Library, 1949.

5. Leonsis, T. *The Business of Happiness: Six Secrets to Extraordinary Success in Life and Work*. Washington, DC: Regnery Publishing, 2010.

6. Reagan, R. "Tear Down This Wall." Fox News. June 1987. http://video.foxnews.com/v/4515392/ronald-reagan-centennial-tear-down-this-wall/.

7. Reagan. "Tear Down This Wall."

8. Denning, S. *The Secret Language of Leadership: How Leaders Inspire Action Through Narrative*. San Francisco: Jossey-Bass, 2007.

Chapter 8

1. Gehrig, L. "Farewell Address." July 1939. http://www.lougehrig.com/about/farewell.html. Lou Gehrig™ is a trademark of the Rip van Winkle Foundation, licensed by CMG Worldwide. www.LouGehrig.com.

2. Gehrig. "Farewell Address."

3. Baseball Almanac. "Lou Gehrig Quotes." http://www.baseball-almanac.com/quotes/quogehr.shtml.

4. Kyi, A.S.S. *Freedom from Fear: And Other Writings*. New York: Penguin, 1991.

5. Friedman, T. "Hard Lines, Red Lines and Green Lines." *New York Times*, September 22, 2012.

6. Savitz, A. W., and Weber, K. *The Triple Bottom Line: How Today's Best-Run Companies Are Achieving Economic, Social, and Environmental Success*. San Francisco: Jossey-Bass, 2006.

7. Zak, P. *The Moral Molecule: The Source of Love and Prosperity*. New York: Penguin, 2012.

8. Valdesolo, P. "Psychologists Uncover Hidden Signals of Trust—Using a Robot." *Scientific American*, Jan. 8, 2013. http://www.scientificamerican.com/article.cfm?id=psychologist-uncover-hidden-signals-of-trust-using-a-robot

9. Friedman. "Hard Lines, Red Lines and Green Lines."

Chapter 9

1. Thomas, B. "What's So Special About Mirror Neurons: Guest blog." *Scientific American*, November 6, 2012.

2. Gordon, R. M. "Radical Simulation." In P. Carruthers and P. K. Smith (eds.), *Theories of Theories of Mind*. Cambridge: Cambridge University Press, 1996.

3. Ramachandran, V. S. *The Neurons that Shaped Civilization*. TED Talks, January 2010.

Chapter 10

1. Bandura, A. "Self Efficacy: Toward a Unifying Theory of Behavioral Change." *Psychological Review*, 1977, *84*(2), 191–215.

2. Thomas, B. "What's So Special About Mirror Neurons." *Scientific American*, November 6, 2012.

3. Hughes, R., Ginnet, R., and Curphy, G. *Leadership: Enhancing the Lessons of Experience*. New York: McGraw-Hill/Irwin, 1993.

Chapter 11

1. Tippett, K. "Listening Beyond Life and Choice." Jan. 20, 2011. http://www.onbeing.org/program/listening-beyond-life-and-choice/transcript/2367.

2. Thatcher, M. "Speech at Kensington Hall ('Britain Awake') (The Iron Lady)." Jan. 19, 1976. http://www.margaretthatcher.org/document/102939

Chapter 12

1. Thompson, D. "Is New Orleans America's Next Great Innovation Hub?" *National Journal*, Apr. 9, 2013. http://www.nationaljournal.com/next-economy/america-360/is-new-orleans-america-s-next-great-innovation-hub-20130409.

2. Britt, R. "New Orleans Business: Most Improved in 2011." *Wall Street Journal*, Dec. 13, 2011.

3. Hamilton, A. "How Louisiana Is Luring Startups." *Time*, Mar. 30, 2012.

Chapter 13

1. DuPont. "Our Vision." 2010. http://www2.dupont.com/corp/en-us/our
-company/vision.html.

2. Maxwell, J. C. "What Are the Five Levels of Leadership?" August
2011. http://johnmaxwellonleadership.com/2011/08/22
/what-are-the-5-levels-of-leadership/.

Conclusion

1. Goodreads. "Anaïs Nin—Quotes—Quotable Quotes." http://www
.goodreads.com/quotes/5030-we-don-t-see-things-as-they-are-we
-see-them.

About the Author

Kathryn D. Cramer, PhD, known among colleagues and clients at The Cramer Institute for her boundless creative energy, is passionate about possibilities and potential. She created and has dedicated her life to asset-based thinking (ABT), a way of looking at the world that helps leaders, influencers, and their teams make small shifts in thinking to produce extraordinary impact. She has worked with clients such as DuPont, Prudential Real Estate, Starbucks, and Microsoft, as well as many educational and nonprofit organizations.

Cramer, a psychologist, has written seven bestselling books, including *Change the Way You See Everything*, which started the ABT global movement. She won an Emmy for her film *Stress: A Personal Challenge*, and was twice featured on the *Oprah Winfrey Show*. She believes in big thinking, the power of presence, and concocting new ideas. She delights in laughter as the great elixir, is inspired by heroic stories of people overcoming adversity, and is on a quest to add the term *asset-based thinking* to the next edition of Merriam-Webster's dictionary.

For more information on The Cramer Institute's signature programs or if you would like to request Cramer for a speaking engagement, please e-mail kcramer@cramerinstitute.com.

Join the Lead Positive Global Community

The more Lead Positive examples we *see* and *say*, the larger the impact of what we *do*. Kathryn Cramer invites you to become part of the burgeoning Lead Positive global movement to reshape the trajectory of leadership. Get inspired by leaders from all walks of life who are bringing out the best in themselves and in their stakeholders and driving positive and transformational change in their organizations. Sign up at drkathycramer.com to join this "positive conspiracy."

Index

Page references followed by *fig* indicate an illustrated figure; followed by *t* indicate a table.

A